ILLUSTRATING EMPIRE

ILLUSTRAT

A VISUAL HISTORY
OF BRITISH IMPERIALISM

Ashley Jackson and David Tomkins

Bodleian Library
UNIVERSITY OF OXFORD

To Kate and Andrea

First published in 2011 by the
Bodleian Library
Broad Street
Oxford OX1 3BG

www.bodleianbookshop.co.uk

ISBN 978 185124 334 1

Text © Ashley Jackson and David Tomkins

Photography © Bodleian Library, University of Oxford, 2011

All images are taken from Bodleian Libraries,
University of Oxford: John Johnson Collection.

This publication has been made possible by a grant from the Scouloudi Foundation
in association with the Institute of Historical Research.

Cover design by Dot Little

Text designed and typeset in 10.5 on 16 ITC Bodoni Twelve
by illuminati, Grosmont

Printed and bound by Great Wall Printing, China

British Library Catalogue in Publishing Data
A CIP record of this publication is available from the British Library

CONTENTS

ACKNOWLEDGEMENTS

We would like to thank Julie Anne Lambert, Librarian of the John Johnson Collection of Printed Ephemera, both for her advice and encouragement, and for making this wonderful collection so readily available to us. Similarly, we are grateful to the project teams at both the Bodleian Library and ProQuest for creating the digital resource *The John Johnson Collection: An Archive of Printed Ephemera*, which allowed us to identify and research much of the material remotely. We would like to thank the staff of the Bodleian Library's Publishing Department, particularly Dr Samuel Fanous, Deborah Susman, Janet Phillips and Su Wheeler; Graham Wilkins, who was responsible for reproducing most of the images in the book; and Dot Little and Lucy Morton, who were responsible for the book's design. The Scouloudi Foundation awarded us a grant towards production costs, and Professor John MacKenzie kindly allowed us to see draft copies of his latest work on popular culture and empire. In attempting to establish the provenance of a particular image, a string of eminent people assisted us, namely Professor Peter Marshall, Professor Sir Christopher Bayly, Dr Anne Marie Misra, Dr Richard Blurton, Dr Peter Carey, Dr Deborah Swallow, Dr Amin Jaffer, Dr Robert Hardgrave, Dr Robert Del Bonta, and Professor Robert Hardgraves. The Defence Studies Department of King's College London generously provided assisted research time for Ashley Jackson during the preparation of this book.

PREFACE

The John Johnson Collection is a treasure trove for historians of eighteenth- to early twentieth-century Britain.

Rich in both images and text, ephemera tell the story of our past through material which is all the more poignant for having survived by chance. Our twenty-first-century minds are constantly challenged and enlightened by glimpses into the daily lives and assumptions of our predecessors. These humble advertisements, handbills, playbills, postcards, street ballads, menus, games, prospectuses, popular prints, bills, labels and posters are not the self-conscious expression of a generation but items that people produced and handled in the course of their daily lives. Wittingly or unwittingly, ephemera express their age, encapsulating its preconceptions, its anxieties and its optimism. We find assumptions which jar with the political correctness of our own society, such as the supremacy of the Caucasian Englishman over the natives of the colonies in an Imperial age. We see the evolving roles of women of all classes and their campaigns for suffrage. We glimpse domestic lives, servants, the advent of gas and electricity and changing fashions in food. We learn how leisure time was spent: at the theatre, in the pleasure garden or learning of faraway places through dioramas and magic-lantern slides.

The Collection in the Bodleian Library, Oxford, assembled by John de Monins Johnson (1882–1956), Printer to the University of Oxford, is one of the world's greatest collections of printed ephemera – in its breadth, and especially in its depth. Detailed cataloguing and digitization have provided the facility to make new links, by searching text and images across many of Johnson's seven hundred subject sections. Able to draw on this enhanced access to the Collection, this new series of books examines different aspects of British social, political and cultural history through the material of the age, helping us to step back in time and to reassess our preconceptions of the Georgians, Victorians or Edwardians through our enjoyment of contemporary images.

More information on the Collection, its digital projects, online exhibitions and access for research is available at www.bodleian.ox.ac.uk/johnson

Julie Anne Lambert
Librarian of the John Johnson Collection

INTRODUCTION

A kaleidoscope of colourful images brought imperial scenes and ideas about the wider world to the British public and their cousins in the settler colonies overseas. Visual representations of empire and non-European scenes permeated British culture, from highbrow art displayed at the Royal Academy to music-hall ditties and advertisements for toiletries. References to empire and the non-European world appeared in a gallimaufry of forms including calendars, playing cards, biscuit tins and exhibition programmes. Such images offered a window on to an exotic world in which white people appeared in a privileged position and non-whites were often caricatured, along with the game-rich, fecund lands in which they lived. These depictions of the world beyond Europe's shores ensured that ideas associated with distant places and strange peoples were domesticated as they were employed to sell soap, attract visitors to museums or champion political causes.

Throughout the nineteenth century, and for much of the twentieth, the British Empire was an established cultural presence. People in Britain and the dominions regularly encountered vivid portrayals of imperial themes. Many of these visual representations were conscious attempts to purvey imperial messages or use imperial imagery for advertising purposes; others were much more incidental. Many images had nothing specifically to do with 'the British Empire', but related to general 'wider world' traditions, of Crusaders and Saracens, perhaps, or of 'Afric's golden sand'.[1] But even though they were not specifically *imperial*, they blended seamlessly into an imperialistic world-view that reflected very pronounced ideas about the exulted place of Britain and the British, as opposed to 'foreigners' and the lands they inhabited. Of course, what people *thought* about such images, if they thought about them at all, is difficult to gauge.

EPHEMERA AND THE BODLEIAN LIBRARY'S JOHN JOHNSON COLLECTION

Often the images were transmitted through media intended to last for a long time, including statuary encountered in the streets and squares of British and colonial cities commemorating soldier-heroes, monarchs or noted aldermen, as well as oil paintings in galleries, or prints and souvenirs intended to adorn mantelpieces. But perhaps the most powerful purveyors of imperial ideas and images were to be found in the realm of 'ephemera'; 'things of short-lived interest', as the *Oxford English Dictionary* defines it, such as political tracts, paper bags, posters, food labels, newspapers and matchboxes. This was because they were so frequently encountered in the quotidian experience of people of all classes.

It is the Bodleian Library's John Johnson Collection of Printed Ephemera, and in particular that material within it which might be seen to reflect imperial themes, which has inspired this book. The word e*phemera* comes from the Greek *ephemeros*, meaning to last for one day. It is generally used to describe material which has been created specifically to last for a finite period and then be discarded; in its printed form, it refers to what Maurice Rickards termed 'the minor transient documents of everyday life'.[2] While such material could well be deemed 'throwaway' in the context of its original purpose, that which survives assumes value when used as documentary evidence that informs our social and cultural history. Ephemera do not always sit comfortably within the collecting policies of libraries, archives or museums, yet they are increasingly gaining credence as primary source materials for academic historical research and an understanding of the past as it was lived by those who were there at the time.

The images presented here have all been taken from the Bodleian Library's John Johnson Collection of Printed Ephemera, which offers diverse ways in which to approach the multifarious aspects of empire and its impact on the everyday lives of those who lived within its bounds. At the beginning of the last century, John de Monins Johnson (1882–1956) had bucked his family's second-son tradition of Cambridge and the church by heading to Oxford to study Classics.[3] Following a brief spell in the Egyptian Civil Service, a burgeoning career in papyrology was curtailed by the outbreak of war in 1914. Johnson, unfit for active service, found himself at Oxford University Press, where, reflecting his future passion for ephemera, he pioneered the use of contemporary documentation in the illustration of history texts for schools.

Having been appointed Printer to the University in 1925, Johnson began to assemble what would ultimately become the greatest collection of printed ephemera in the country, if not the world. He was a voracious but discriminate collector, notable (if not unique) in that, while others might concentrate on collecting cigarette cards, theatre playbills or beer labels, Johnson retrospectively collected all and every type of ephemeral printing, eventually amassing over a million items,

Stanley in Africa, c. 1890s.

A dramatic battle scene from a magazine (Dean's Gold Medal Series No. 14) which presented stereotypical images of Africa and Africans and the role of explorers and missionaries in their midst. In a manner typical of the era, and now widely discredited, it glorifies the expeditions of the explorer and journalist Henry Morton Stanley.

JJ Empire & Colonies 5

ith Mazembani's ... people

which he grouped under some seven hundred headings according to subject. Transferred from the University Press in 1968, the Collection has been in the care of the Bodleian Library for some forty years, where its successive custodians have striven both to preserve and to expand this unique record of the commonplace and the remarkable. Though there are items that date to the year Michelangelo first climbed a ladder in the Sistine Chapel, the Collection is strongest with regard to the eighteenth, nineteenth and twentieth centuries. As Graham Hudson asserts, 'Produced to meet the needs of the passing day, in content and form ephemera are wholly part of the culture in which they are created.'[4] It is hardly surprising, therefore, that so much of the John Johnson Collection's material that dates from this era is suffused with the presence of empire. It must be stressed, in anticipation of the question 'Where are the non-European images and perspectives?', that the John Johnson Collection is overwhelmingly concerned with British – and therefore white, 'metropolitan' – images.

This type of material is exciting because it is relatively unknown. We know a lot about the literature, the music and the art of empire. For literature, we have the well-known genres represented by Rudyard Kipling, H. Rider Haggard, E.M. Forster and the *Boy's Own Paper*. For the soundtrack of empire, we think of composers and musicians such as Elgar or Gilbert and Sullivan, and patriotic or martial tunes performed on bandstands and quarterdecks. Art and empire usually stirs thoughts of canvases showing cavalry charges in distant places or 'Sons of the Blood'-style paintings with clear patriotic intent. Since the 1980s popular culture has been an important aspect of academic research on empire, though visual studies have been few and far between, and the imagery and iconography of empire and its ephemeral manifestations insufficiently understood. In short, there has been a lot *said* about culture and empire, but not a great deal *seen*; the written word has triumphed over the visual image. In this book, the powerful and often complex images that conveyed information and ideas about empire and the non-European world are allowed to speak for themselves.

Studying visual representations of empire helps us develop a more nuanced assessment of what the British Empire was, and how attitudes towards empire and foreign lands and peoples were shaped. Concrete manifestations of empire – war memorials, statues, Empire Day pageants, the Empire (later Commonwealth) Games, empire exhibitions – need to be understood alongside less obvious protrusions of empire into people's lives. This is because they influenced people's views, lent the Empire popular support, and created a bank of common cultural references. These included Jack Tar and Tommy Atkins, 'loyal' as well as 'barbaric' natives, wily Orientals, and redoubtable missionaries. They also included untamed landscapes of desert, jungle and mountains.

An awareness of popular culture and imperial imagery enables us to understand the Empire as a fluid and complex entity in the minds of individual people, as much an inchoate, even fantasy, construct as it was the firmly bounded physical entity depicted in world maps showing the Empire in red. Such illustrations 'remind us what a complex, multi-faceted institution the Empire was: part big business, part military machine, part potent vehicle for advertising, part cultural centrepiece, part mass employer and a form of social services, part enforcer of ethnic stereotypes, part entertainer, part a booster of national self-confidence, and much more besides'.[5] As the images in this volume show, the Empire was portrayed in diverse ways, and this was done in an imaginative and often light-hearted manner. The range of images considered is testament to the sophistication of advertisers, artists and designers of bygone years, as well as to the complexity of the imperial experience for the colonizers as well as the colonized. Illustrations of empire were often beguiling. They largely rendered empire and European supremacy as good, not bad; they presented actions and attitudes which today are considered highly controversial or even wicked in a positive light, such as to make them appear acceptable, even normal. This book contains some images which today appear highly offensive, illustrating notions about peoples and places which are inaccurate and discredited. Such images, however, serve as informative primary source material which helps us to understand British attitudes and perceptions of the time.

The study of imperial imagery, particularly ephemera, serves another important function. It emphasizes the fact that the British Empire, and the engagement of Britain with the non-European world, is an integral part of British history. Empire is seldom properly connected to the metropolitan history of Britain, despite the intensive efforts of some historians; but, as these images show, it was a central cultural presence that embraced a multitude of key economic, political and social issues. To say that attitudes towards empire were ambivalent, or that many people were ignorant about it,

'Empire Day', *c.* 1901–11.

This postcard shows the different peoples of the Empire surrounding a monument to the late Queen, with a picture of her son and successor Edward VII, and a stirring patriotic message ('One King, One Flag, One Fleet, One Empire'). Empire Day was held on 24 May, Queen Victoria's birthday.

JJ John Fraser Collection: Propaganda: GB (3)

rather misses the point. A modern example might be employed to illustrate. Today, some people in Britain, Poland, Egypt or Indonesia might be ambivalent towards America, and even ignorant about it. But they will all have an impression of that country and what it represents, and will have been touched by its political, economic, military and cultural power. Many other people in those countries, of course, will have very sharply defined impressions of America, usually a mixture of good impressions and bad ones. Such was the awareness of the British Empire, a global hegemon whose weight was felt, in one way or another, by millions of people around the world.

THE EMPIRE AS EVERYDAY

The British Empire, and a view of the wider world and Britain's place within it, became part of the furniture of British life, and the Empire was a defining presence on the international stage. That is not to say that people were necessarily interested in or knowledgeable about empire or distant lands and peoples, or that their views were accurate or homogenized; it is simply to say that there was such a barrage of information that it was difficult to avoid imbibing. Even things that had nothing consciously to do with an imperialized world frequently sent imperial signals or made reference to a view of Britain and its place in the world that had become common currency through repetition.

A good example of empire and imperial themes appearing in the distinctly non-imperial lives of real people is provided by that renowned chronicler of English rural life, Flora Thompson. In her tales of the hamlet of Juniper Hill, better known by the fictional name of Lark Rise, Thompson recorded the permeation of empire into the countryside during the 1880s.[6] Into her isolated rural community – a hamlet marooned amidst the cornfields of Oxfordshire – came soldiers home from Egypt and India bearing stories, trinkets and a whiff of adventure. 'Nearly every family in the hamlet had its soldier son or uncle or cousin', Thompson wrote, 'and it was a common sight to see a scarlet coat going round the Rise.'[7] The celebration of Queen Victoria's Golden Jubilee in 1887 was an unparalleled event in the hamlet's history, as it was for communities throughout the land. Common consumer items bore imperial marks, such as 'Nigger Head' tobacco and tins of Australian rabbit sold by the innkeeper's wife. The baker, a ship's carpenter by trade, remained a sailor at heart and would tell Laura (the fictional name Flora Thompson adopted in the book) and her siblings of piling seas, shipwreck, islands and palm

A colourful illustration for Nabob cigars, *c.* 1910–20.

JJ Labels 22 (23a)

trees, and 'treacherous little men living in palm leaf huts, their faces brown as your frock, Laura'.[8] Maps on the schoolroom wall offered 'fascinating descriptions of such far-apart places as Greenland and the Amazon; of the Pacific Ocean with its fairy islands and coral reefs; the snows of Hudson Bay Territory and the sterile heights of the Andes. Best of all she loved the descriptions of the Himalayas, which began: "Northward of the great plain of India, and along its whole extent, towers the sublime mountain region of the Himalayas."'[9] Here, then, we encounter perhaps the three most powerful vectors of imperial ideas and images of the non-European world: word-of-mouth tales and anecdotes, national events and the ephemera of everyday life.

IMAGERY IN PRINT, FILM AND MERCHANDISE

The British public, therefore, was exposed to images of empire and the non-European world through a surprising range of media. There was literature in all its forms, including a constant tide of ephemeral writing in comics, newspapers, magazines and the journals of well-known and obscure organizations, such as *The British Emigrant* and *The Imperial Colonist*, and the quarterly publications of organizations such as the Royal Over-Seas League and the Round Table. Illustrated newspapers, magic lantern (a lamp projecting slide images) displays and artists' impressions helped people visualize the Empire. There was also the great encyclopaedia projects in which the British showed off their knowledge of other people's lands. Another distinct literary category was material produced during political campaigns. Topics such as imperial federation, Irish Home Rule, the plight of Chinese labourers in South Africa, slavery and the opium trade were common subjects.

Other media that conveyed imperial messages included music, films, theatre and painting. There were also manufactured physical

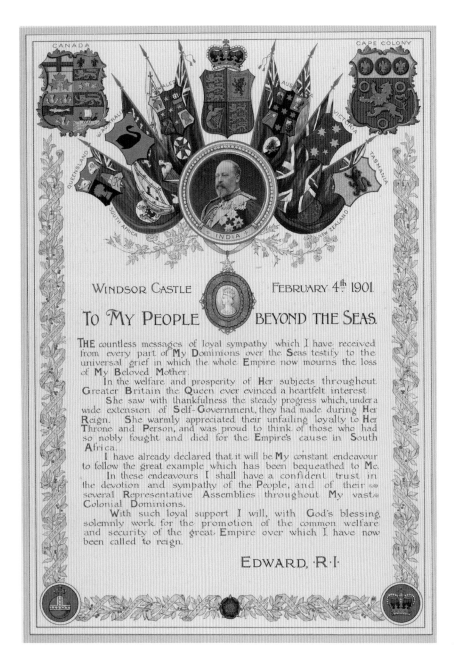

WINDSOR CASTLE   FEBRUARY 4th 1901.

TO MY PEOPLE   BEYOND THE SEAS.

THE countless messages of loyal sympathy which I have received from every part of My Dominions over the Seas testify to the universal grief in which the whole Empire now mourns the loss of My Beloved Mother.

In the welfare and prosperity of Her subjects throughout Greater Britain the Queen ever evinced a heartfelt interest. She saw with thankfulness the steady progress which, under a wide extension of Self-Government, they had made during Her Reign. She warmly appreciated their unfailing loyalty to Her Throne and Person, and was proud to think of those who had so nobly fought and died for the Empire's cause in South Africa.

I have already declared that it will be My constant endeavour to follow the great example which has been bequeathed to Me.

In these endeavours I shall have a confident trust in the devotion and sympathy of the People, and of their several Representative Assemblies throughout My vast Colonial Dominions.

With such loyal support I will, with God's blessing, solemnly work for the promotion of the common welfare and security of the great Empire over which I have now been called to reign.

EDWARD. R·I·

'To My People Beyond the Seas'.

A message to the Empire from the new King, Edward VII, dated 4 February 1901, two days after his mother's funeral. Victoria died on 22 January with her son and her grandson, the German Emperor Wilhelm II, at her bedside. As she disliked black funerals, London was draped in purple and white as she was laid to rest beside her husband Albert in Windsor Great Park.

JJ Empire & Colonies 1

objects connected with national and imperial events that bore messages concerning the non-European world and Britain's place in it. These included jubilee mugs, ashtrays, souvenirs, gifts brought back from overseas, statues, headstones and brass plaques commemorating imperial figures, as well as decorative street furniture such as drinking fountains. Other objects included children's games with imperial themes, and even coins; in the twentieth century the words 'King of all the Britons, Emperor of India' appeared on all British pennies, and the guinea was the principal gold unit from 1663 until 1813, the name referring to the West African region where the gold originated.

Museum collections, exhibitions, waxworks, and attractions such as 'convict' ships provided another category of popular culture through which empire and imperial themes were put 'on show'. There were also ephemera associated with commerce and marketing

Goldrush in Australia.

A sketch from a series of 1853 images depicting life on the Australian goldfields, drawn 'on the spot' by Samuel Thomas Gill.

JJ Empire & Colonies 1

'Eat Australian fruit and dairy produce', *c.* **1930s.**

A selection from a series of colourful booklets advertising Australian fruit, vegetables and dairy produce aimed at the British market.

JJ Emigration 1

– 'consumer empire' – that included food labels, trade fair catalogues, marketing campaigns and a galaxy of advertisements which associated consumer products with imperial and wider world themes. Such products included beer, tobacco, tinned fruit, sugar, rubber goods, cars, tropical clothing and ocean cruises. Imperial themes were a marketing man's dream; they could be used to conjure almost any sensation or desire.

The colonies themselves contributed to this outpouring of imagery. Governments in New Zealand or Canada targeted the British public through alluring brochures and posters, enticing them to visit for holidays or offering them land on which to settle. Landmark occasions in the history of individual colonies or colonial cities led to a flowering of ephemera, as settler communities celebrated their progress made in building new nations (usually, of course, at the expense of pre-existing non-European ones). As decolonization gathered pace new countries published souvenir handbooks celebrating 'Merdeka' or 'Uhuru', marking the event with new national flags, commemorative stamps and new coats of arms – often designed in Britain and representing an interesting blend of the traditional and the new, ensuring that enduring, if sometimes unintended, links remained between the 'mother country' and its erstwhile colonies.

IMPERIALISM IN BRITISH CULTURE: THE DEBATE

Illustrating Empire examines the cultural depiction of the British Empire, including emigration and overseas settlement, the Empire's political obtrusions, the methods of imperial governance, the role of religion and exploration in cementing colonial control, the impact of empire on popular culture and the networks of imperial travel and trade. The book does not seek to take sides in the academic debate that centres upon the extent to which British society was, or was not, affected by imperial ideas. According to some historians, British society was saturated with imperial references, and the public 'steeped' in awareness of the Empire and its major themes. Others, however, sharply disagree with this interpretation, arguing that *ignorance* of empire was a much more notable trend. According to this latter view, though there were imperial references in British culture, they only amounted to a fraction of the cultural output with which the public was presented. Furthermore, just because imperial propagandists might portray imperial themes in their work, it did not necessarily mean that the public internalized their messages. The main proponent of this view, Bernard Porter, entitled a research paper 'Empire? What Empire?'[10] The Empire, according to this view, was far from all-pervasive in the lives of the British people, and played little part in their sense of national identity, at least not until the jingoism of the late nineteenth century associated with the rise of the German 'menace' and increased foreign competition. Growing up in London in the 1940s and 1950s, Ronald Hyam claims that 'if you had asked us about the Empire, we would have assumed you meant the Chiswick Empire, a music hall two miles down the road.'[11] Overseas, meanwhile, whilst white settlers had a developed sense of the Empire by virtue of their decision to leave the British Isles, many of Britain's non-European subjects had little awareness of the fact that they were British subjects at all.

On the other side of the debate, the leading scholar is John MacKenzie.[12] He has dominated a field of scholarship addressing imperialism and popular culture since the publication of two landmark studies, *Propaganda and Empire: The Manipulation of British Public Opinion, 1880–1960* (1984) and *Imperialism and Popular Culture* (1986).[13] These volumes became the pioneering texts

'A new life in the colonies'.

An emigration brochure from the interwar period advertising opportunities for overseas settlement.

JJ Emigration 3

in a 'Studies in Imperialism' series that in 2009 numbered nearly ninety titles. The themes the series has addressed give a flavour of the aspects of society and culture that the Empire influenced. They include medicine, armed forces, police, exhibitions, the environment, museums, children's literature, citizenship, migration, sexuality, gender, race, education, the stage, air power, advertising, cities, science, music, the media, childhood, sport, travel and products such as chocolate, jute and silk.[14] For MacKenzie's side of the debate, imperialism was 'a dominant idea and force of the age', and imperial history demands to be understood as a part of British domestic history. As MacKenzie writes, 'the fact is that imperial events slotted into an exciting adventure and militarist tradition which translated readily into other media, not just the stage and the press, but also popular literature, painting, prints, statuary, memorials, and music.'[15] Knowledge of empire was enhanced by the phenomenon of migration that took nearly twenty million Britons overseas, as well as the work of Christian missions and youth organizations such as the Boy Scouts. This further blended with an awareness (though not, of course, a universal detailed knowledge) of central imperial fantasies and self-justificatory myths, such as the alleged importance of empire in spreading knowledge, freedom, prosperity and peace.

Whilst seeking not to take sides in this debate, *Illustrating Empire* argues, on the basis of visual evidence, that a vast range of ephemera was put before the British public that made reference to imperial and non-European themes. The distinction is an important one: whilst some of the images and publications considered were not *specifically* related to territories of the British Empire or acts of British imperialism, they all refer to the non-European world and purveyed a range of common views about non-European peoples and lands in relation to European peoples. Perhaps the answer to the 'empire and popular culture' conundrum is that whilst most Britons may not have been 'imperially minded' or knowledgeable about the Empire unless it directly touched their lives, a vast range of cultural references shaped people's background ideas about foreigners, especially non-European foreigners, and Britain's (and Britons') place in the world.

To conclude, we offer a medley of imperial and wider world themes drawn at random from the John Johnson Collection. It illustrates the manner in which the Empire was put before the British public. In April 1836 newspapers carried adverts for a new attraction at the 'African Glen' at the Coliseum in Regent's Park, offering 'views across the New British Settlement of Graham's Town, South Africa's Great Karroo, or desert, Cape Town and Table Bay'.[16] In 1850 Portland Gallery at Langham Place in London displayed an elaborate 'Diorama of the Ganges',[17] and five years later the Egyptian Hall, Piccadilly, was showing 'grand moving panoramic pictures of the Nile'.[18] In 1859 the Egyptian Hall was showing 'To China and Back', the illustrated travelogue of Albert Smith.[19] Moving into the twentieth century, in the interwar years an advertising campaign encouraged British shoppers to 'Eat Canadian "Beekist" Honey' and 'Keep Empire Bees Busy'.[20] In 1953, British investors were invited to put their money in Jamaica because of its 'pioneer taxation relief, expanding Caribbean markets, and proximity to the dollar market'.[21] Whether you were going to the theatre in the mid-nineteenth century, eating honey in the interwar years, or seeking investment opportunities in the year of Elizabeth II's coronation, the British Empire and the non-European world were likely to be encountered, in one form or another.

EMPIRE, SETTLEMENT AND EMIGRATION

The growth of the British Empire changed the map of the world and its racial demographics, and the migration of people was central to these processes. The settler phenomenon, which embraced American expansion into the 'wild west' as well as the arrival of convicts in New South Wales, shaped the modern world and continues to resonate. Millions of people left the British Isles and began new lives in the 'neo-Britains' of America, Australia, Canada, New Zealand and South Africa. It is no surprise, therefore, that emigration and settlement have left a large volume of printed ephemera. It includes government forms for settlers seeking entry into Australia, reports and pictures relating to emigrant ships or colonial gold strikes, engravings depicting scenes from new overseas settlements and posters reminding the British public that the purchase of Cape fruit or New Zealand lamb was patriotic and helped reduce unemployment. In addition to out-migration from Britain, human traffic associated with the British Empire included slavery and indentured labour. The evil transatlantic trade in humans produced ephemera of its own in the form of political and religious tracts, bills of sale, advertisements for runaway slaves, printed songs, anti-slavery ceramic cameos and tokens, and glazed pottery jugs.

A range of private and personal factors – from famine and fortune-hunting to religious persecution or zeal – led people to emigrate. So, too, did government- and royal-sponsored initiatives. King Charles II gave William Penn a huge tract of land in order to secure Quakers from persecution; Georgia was established as a debtors' colony; penal settlements were formed in New South Wales and Tasmania; and governments offered assisted passage and free land in order to relieve Britain of 'overpopulation' and build up British stock in colonies seeking to expand.

The displacement of people from Britain to other parts of the world was invariably accompanied by the dispossession of indigenous inhabitants. This was the very essence of colonialism (or 'settlerism' as it has been termed); people on the ground in other lands making it 'theirs', usually at the expense of inhabitants already resident. This was as much a product of the multifarious activities of individuals and private interest groups, such as settlement orchestrated by the British South Africa Company in Rhodesia, as it was a product of government-sponsored endeavour. From the moment Europeans arrived, indigenes were increasingly subjected to their economic and political domination, often by military means, and their ownership of land and the means of production heavily circumscribed.

The imposition of white rule saw the appropriation of indigenous culture as well as land and power. The new rulers claimed to understand it better or to be able to 'restore' it to supposed former glories, documenting it and even removing ancestral artefacts and skeletons for analysis, preservation and display in the great museums and laboratories of Edinburgh or London. Native Americans or Canadians were indeed the 'first peoples', as were Australian Aboriginals, New Zealand Maoris, Palestinian Arabs, Kikuyu, Maasai and San. But they were soon second-class citizens, and the new settler societies emerged largely at their expense. Subsequent wars of 'pacification' or 'counter-insurgency' usually had their roots in this fundamental fact of overseas settlement: dispossession and the usurpation of political control by aliens. 'Indian' wars in North America, Maori wars in New Zealand, 'Kaffir' wars in South Africa, the 'Chimurenga' in Southern Rhodesia and Mau Mau in Kenya – all were wars of settlement and colonization.

Despite these stark facts, few British people left their native shores intent upon dispossessing others. Places such as Australia or Canada were presented as vast open spaces just waiting for people to turn their dormant pastures into productive agricultural estates. The settler societies marketed themselves as sunny, prosperous 'Britains', where emigrants could build new lives and new towns whilst contributing to the complementary growth of a global economy in which Britain, with its industry and insatiable appetite for raw materials and food, dovetailed with fledgling settler societies seeking markets for their wool or wheat. New Zealand described itself variously as 'the Empire's dairy farm' and 'Britain in the South'. Southern Rhodesia was the 'land of sunshine', and Victoria was Australia's 'garden state'. Canada was portrayed as a land overflowing with infeasibly large carrots and other fruit and vegetables, as well as vast fertile plains. As the settler colonies improved their image, which had previously been associated with inhospitable environments, criminality and economic failure at home, propaganda emphasized the positive benefits of living overseas. Negative aspects were papered over: the Canadian weather, for example, went from freezing cold to 'bracing'.

In the nineteenth century there were both 'free' settlers – often moving overseas as part of 'model colonization' programmes intended to create idyllic, socially balanced communities in the new world – and forced migrants, transported to the other side of the world for crimes committed in Britain. In the twentieth century, these free and unfree migratory trends continued. On the one hand, ex-servicemen were actively encouraged to contribute to the development of vigorous new settler states, particularly in the would-be dominions Kenya and Southern Rhodesia. On the other hand, as late as the 1960s tens of thousands of children from British orphanages and care homes were sent to Australia and other settler colonies.

The phenomenon of migration led to the growth of new cities and ports, political institutions and Western modes of living in distinctly non-Western environments. Wherever settlers appeared in number, Western-style buildings and urban spaces soon emerged. The 'universal' bungalow, the cathedrals of Montreal, the quadrangle of Sydney University, the Victoria Falls Bridge, colonial Williamsburg, the botanical gardens of Christchurch, New Zealand, and the national parks of South Africa – all are testament to the spread of settlers and their impact upon the built and natural environments.

According to the historian Stuart Ward, 'An apparently thriving empire promoted the idea of a world-wide British identity – the myth of a Greater Britain – that resonated at all levels of metropolitan culture'.[1] The existence of this 'British world' became a core aspect of a shared world-view, and was referred to in a range of ephemeral publications. Having relatives in Canada or South Africa, eating New Zealand lamb or butter and sending sports teams to tour the 'white' Commonwealth were all part of the British experience in the twentieth century. Among settler communities overseas an awareness of 'home' was built into nascent national identities that remained imperial even whilst they were becoming more localized (though this was not necessarily the case among white settlers of non-British stock, such as the Afrikaners or the Québécois). The Irish formed a distinct strand of emigration and settlement, creating a strong diaspora. The monarch's Christmas broadcast to the Empire, initiated in the early 1930s, emphasized a sense of global community, as did advertisements in publications such as the Army and Navy Stores catalogues that reminded people to order early for Christmas if they wanted to send gifts to friends and family overseas. Shipping parcels indicated the growth of overseas communities tied to Britain. In 1909, 277,549 parcels were shipped to India and 123,656 received from the subcontinent. In the same year 244,510 parcels were sent to South Africa, 155,246 to Australia and New Zealand, and 314,731 to Canada.[2] This sense of a global community, supported by official and personal networks, was further emphasized by the commemoration of those who fell during the Empire's wars.

The images in this chapter address themes such as the departure of settlers from Britain; scenes of early colonial life relayed to curious people back in Britain through engravings, sketches, lithographs and paintings; and references to emigration in organs such as the *Illustrated London News*. Newspapers depicted departing Britons and their possessions mustering at the docks. Through various media, the British public was regaled with information about colonial life, such as the 'diggings' in Australia, scenes of 'life in the Cape', and feature articles such as *The Graphic*'s 'Byways of New Zealand'. Thus new frontiers were put before the public and new knowledge accrued.

The high levels of emigration led to the formation of interest groups such as the British Women's Emigration Association and numerous publications dedicated to the worldwide community of British settlers, including *The Imperial Colonist* and the *Imperial and Colonial Magazine*. These organizations and their journals had a variety of agendas or causes to champion, from the blatantly nationalistic and Social Darwinistic to those associated with morality or the development of the Empire as an economic unit.

The growth of settler societies and of new towns and cities featuring Western-style architecture were marked on anniversaries such as Vancouver's diamond jubilee in 1946, the Canadian confederation's diamond jubilee in 1927 and Australia's 150th anniversary celebrations in 1938. The dominions also had their own exhibitions – for which stunning buildings, such as Melbourne's Royal Victoria Exhibition Centre, were erected. These events celebrated the colonialists' view of how modernity had sprung from 'wilderness' and how far young settler societies had 'progressed'.

N.B.—This Half Sheet to be kept by the Applicant

AUSTRALIA.

GOVERNMENT EMIGRATION OFFICE,
8, PARK STREET, WESTMINSTER.

REGULATIONS
FOR THE SELECTION OF EMIGRANTS, AND CONDITIONS ON WHICH PASSAGES ARE GRANTED.

QUALIFICATIONS OF EMIGRANTS

1. The Emigrants must be of those callings which, from time to time, are most in demand in the Colony. They must be sober, industrious, of general good moral character, *and have been in the habit of working for wages ;*—of all of which decisive certificates will be required. They must also be in good health, free from all bodily or mental defects ; and the Adults must, in all respects, be capable of labour, and going out to work for wages, at the occupation specified on their Application Forms. The Candidates who will receive a preference are respectable young women trained to domestic or farm service, and families in which there is a preponderance of females.

2. The separation of husbands and wives, and of parents from children under 18 will in no case be allowed.

3. Single women, under 18, cannot be taken without their parents, unless they go under the immediate care of some near relatives. Single women with illegitimate children can in no case be taken.

4. Single men cannot be taken, unless they are sons in eligible Families, containing at least a corresponding number of daughters.

5. Families in which there are more than two children under seven years of age,—or in which the sons outnumber the daughters ;—Widowers and Widows with young children ;—Persons who intend to *resort to the gold fields,* to buy land, or to invest capital, in trade ;—or who are in the habitual receipt of parish relief ;—or who have not been vaccinated, or not had the small-pox ; cannot be accepted.

APPLICATION AND APPROVAL.

6. Applications must be made to the Commissioners in the Form annexed. The filling up of the Form, is merely to bring the applicant's case fully before the Board. It confers no claim to a passage ; and implies no pledge that the Candidates, though within the Regulations, will be accepted ; for as the applications are usually more numerous than the Emigration Funds can meet, only the most desirable even of eligible candidates can be chosen.

7. From the number of applications, some time must necessarily elapse after the Form is sent in before it can be considered. If approved of, the Applicants will receive a printed "Approval Circular," calling for the Contribution required by Article 8, and pointing out how the money is to be paid. After it is paid, they will, as soon as the Commissioners' arrangements will permit, receive an Embarkation Order *(which is not transferable),* naming the Ship in which they are to embark, and the time and place of joining her. *Applicants must not leave their homes before the receipt of this Order.*

PAYMENTS TOWARDS PASSAGES.

8. The Contributions above-mentioned (out of which the Commissioners provide Bedding and Mess Utensils, &c., for the Voyage,) are as follows :—

CLASSES	Under 45	45 and under 50	50 and under 60
	£	£	£
I. Married Agricultural Labourers, Shepherds, Herdsmen, and their Wives; (for South Australia Copper Miners also,) and Women of the Working Class—per Head	1	5	11
II. Married Journeymen Mechanics and Artizans—such as Blacksmiths, Bricklayers, Carpenters, Masons, Sawyers, Wheelwrights, Gardeners, &c. and their Wives, per Head	2	6	14
III. Single Men, subject to the conditions in Article 4, and if accompanying their Parents	2		
IV. Children under 14—per Head	10		

Passages from Dublin and Cork to Plymouth, from Glasgow to Liverpool, and from Granton Pier to London are provided by the Commissioners for Emigrants. All other travelling expenses must be borne

CAUTIONS TO APPLICANTS.

9. *No preparations must on any account be made by the Applicants, either by withdrawing from employment or otherwise, until they receive the "Approval Circular."* Applicants who fail to attend to this warning will do so at their own risk, and will have no claim whatever on the Commissioners.

10. The Selecting Agents of the Board have no authority to promise passages in any case, nor to receive money. *If, therefore, Applicants wish to make their payments through the Agents, instead of in the manner pointed out in the "Approval Circular," they must understand that they do so at their own risk, and that the Commissioners will in no way be responsible.*

11. Should any Signatures attached to an Applicant's paper prove to be not genuine, or any personation be attempted, or any false representations be made in the papers, not only will the application be rejected, and the contribution forfeited, but the offenders will be liable, under the Passengers' Act, to a PENALTY NOT EXCEEDING £50.

12. Should any Applicants be found on personal examination at the Depôt, or on Board, to have made any mis-statement in their papers, or to have omitted to state any material fact, or to have any infectious disorder, or otherwise not to be in a fit state of health for the voyage, or to have any mental or bodily defect likely to impair their usefulness as labourers, or to have left any of their young Children behind, or to have brought with them more Children than are mentioned in their Application Form, or expressly sanctioned by the Commissioners, or to have attempted any deception whatever, or evasion of these Rules, they will be refused admission on board the Ship, or if embarked, will be landed, without having any claim on the Commissioners. If after embarkation Emigrants are guilty of insubordination, or misconduct, they will be relanded, and forfeit their Contributions.

13. If Applicants fail to attend at the appointed time and place for embarkation, without having previously given to the Commissioners timely notice, and a satisfactory reason,—or if they fail to proceed in the Ship,—or are rejected for any of the reasons specified in the preceding article, they will forfeit their contributions, and will have no claim to a passage at any future time.

OUTFIT, &c.

14. The Commissioners supply, free of charge, Provisions, Medical Attendance, and Cooking Utensils at their Depôt and on board the Ship. Also, new Mattresses, Bolsters, Blankets, and Counterpanes, Canvas Bags to contain Linen, &c., Knives and Forks, Spoons, Metal Plates, and Drinking Mugs, which articles will be given after arrival in the Colony to the Emigrants who have behaved well on the voyage.

15. The Emigrants must bring their own Clothing, which will be inspected at the Port by an Officer of the Commissioners ; and they will not be allowed to embark unless they have a sufficient stock for the voyage, not less, for each Person, than—

FOR MALES.	FOR FEMALES.
Six Shirts	Six Shifts
Six pairs Stockings	Two Flannel Petticoats
Two ditto Shoes	Six pairs Stockings
Two complete suits of exterior Clothing.	Two ditto Shoes
	Two Gowns.

With at least 3 Sheets for each berth, and 4 Towels and 2 lbs. of Soap for each person. But the larger the stock of Clothing the better for health and comfort during the voyage, which usually lasts about four months, and as the Emigrants have always to pass through very hot and very cold weather, they should be prepared for both ; 2 or 3 Serge Shirts for Men, and Flannel for Women and Children, are strongly recommended.

16. The Emigrants should take out with them the necessary tools of their Trades that are not bulky. But the whole quantity of baggage for each Adult must not measure more than 20 cubic or solid feet, nor exceed half a ton in weight. It must be packed in one or more boxes ; but no box must exceed in size 10 cubic feet. Large packages and extra baggage, if it can be taken at all, must be paid for. Mattresses and feather beds will in no case be taken.

17. The Emigrants will have to sign a written engagement at the port of embarkation, *that if they go to the gold fields, or if they quit the Colony within 4 years after landing, they must repay to the Colonial Government a proportionate part of their Passage-money, at the rate of £4 per Adult, for each year wanting to complete four years from landing.*

18. All Applications should be addressed, Post-paid to S. Walcott,

An illustration from the *Illustrated London News*, 7 May 1870, showing the ship *Ganges*.

The ship departed from Victoria Docks with 761 emigrants for Canada, many of them from the East End Emigration Club. *Ganges* left London on 28 April destined for Quebec and Montreal, arriving on 15 May. During the voyage one person died, another was born, and the ship landed with a minor outbreak of measles and smallpox on board. In the year 1870 alone, 44,475 immigrants landed in Quebec, 33,073 of them having come from Britain.

JJ Emigration Folder

DEPARTURE OF EMIGRANTS FOR CANADA

The Ganges, a fine screw-steamer, of 1899 tons register, W. S. Mason, commander, left the Victoria Docks, on Wednesday week, at eleven o'clock, having on board a large party of emigrants connected with the East-End Emigration Club, a society acting in union with the committee of the British and Colonial Emigration Fund. Of the entire number of 761 souls who were on the lists as going by this ship, only four were wanting at the moment the vessel cast off from the quay. Among the parties present to witness the departure of the emigrants were Lord and Lady Alfred Churchill, Sir T. Fowell Buxton; Mr. Andrew Johnston, M.P.; the Rev. J. F. and Mrs. Kitto, the Rev. W. J. Caparn, Mr. E. H. Currie, and others. The Rev. J. Cohen, Rector of Whitechapel, was also on board, going in the vessel to Canada as chaplain, in company with Mrs. Cohen. Captain Forster, R.N., the chief emigration inspector for the port of London, was present in discharge of his official duties, and no effort seemed to be wanting to secure the comfort of the passengers. Close at hand, the screw-steamer Tweed, belonging to Messrs. Temperley's line of packets, displayed her bunting in gay profusion, being herself destined to start for Canada next morning with another large party of emigrants, under the auspices of the same societies. Besides the visitors on board the Ganges, many of whom accompanied the vessel as far down the river as Gravesend, a number of working people lined the adjacent quays, manifesting a lively interest in the proceedings, and cheering loudly as the Ganges proceeded out of dock. The emigrants were somewhat superior to the usual class, a circumstance partly attributable to the fact that they themselves contributed to the cost of their passage at the rate of £3 per statute adult. The actual cost of sending out this ship-load of emigrants will be rather more than £3400, exclusive of a sum of £1142, which has been advanced from Kelsall's Emigration Charity, to meet the expenses of an outfit, and to give the emigrant a start on his landing. The obvious deficit has been made up in various ways. Public subscriptions to the club have added £200 to the members' payments; the Poplar Board of Guardians has contributed a further sum of £100; assistance has also been given from the Manufacturers' Relief Fund; and the balance has been met by the British and Colonial Emigration Fund, of which the Lord Mayor is president, and towards which the Right Hon. G. J. Goschen, M.P., and his brother have each contributed £1000.

The Darien Canal project has been rejected by the Columbian Congress, notwithstanding the favourable terms which Columbia was supposed to have made.

EMIGRANTS BY THE SHIP GANGES DEPARTING FOR CANADA.

THE THEATRES.

Messrs. Mansell are active managers. On Monday they strengthened the usual attractions at the Lyceum by the production of a new operetta, graced with the music of Offenbach, entitled "Breaking the Spell." The plot is exceedingly simple, and the characters few. These consist of a Chelsea pensioner, an amorous gardener, and a soubrette. The two latter have had a lovers' quarrel, and Peter Bloom (Mr. G. F. Neville), in a fit of desperation, has enlisted for a soldier. He attributes this rash act to the influence exerted on his mind by old Matthews's violin, which set him dancing, and deprived him of judgment. Old Matthews (Mr. Aynsley Cook) regrets the circumstances, and seeks to remedy it by applying to the Duke of Marlborough for his discharge, leaving his fiddle in the custody of Jemmy Wood (Miss S. Dolaro). While he is gone, Peter Bloom, in a rage, breaks the fatal instrument. Great are the lamentations of the old man, when he returns; but Bloom, taking up the fragments, finds an inclosure consisting of a letter and a hundred-pound note. With this Bloom's discharge can be purchased, and a balance besides of sixty pounds secured, to make all parties happy. The music is sparkling, lively, and effective; and the acting all that could be desired. It is illustrated with a scene painted by Mr. Hanns, representing Chelsea Hospital on the banks of the Thames, which is well painted, and skilfully set.

The field of theatrical speculation is enlarging on all sides; and, notwithstanding the number of new and commodious theatres which have been lately opened, smaller houses, long neglected, come into the market, and obtain encouragement.

Dr. Sedgwick-Saunders, chairman of the Special Library Committee, has presented to the Court of Common Council a report relative to the new library and museum which are to be erected on land belonging to the Corporation, and adjacent to the Guildhall, at an expense of £25,000. The report stated that the committee directed the City architect (Mr. Horace Jones) to prepare a plan and design, and they now submitted the designs and models which had been prepared by him. They recommended that muniment-rooms should be provided in a portion of the basement of the building at an expense not exceeding £2800. The building will not only be of an ornate character, but will harmonise with the Guildhall and the adjacent property. The library proper will be reached from Basinghall-street, and will be on the upper floor. It will be 98 ft. long, 65 ft. wide, and 40 ft. high, and will be divided into three aisles, the centre being 33 ft. wide. In each of the side aisles there will be seven bays 12 ft. wide and 16 ft. deep; and it is also proposed to construct galleries. The centre aisle will hold at least 1000 persons, and will be connected by a corridor with the dais in the great hall. Below the library will be the museum, a room 82 ft. long, 19 ft. high, and 65 ft. wide. The latter room would be only 7 ft. beneath the level of the street, and a good light would thus be easily obtained. A committee-room is on each floor. Adjoining the library will be a public reading-room, a want long felt by the citizens of London. The report was adopted unanimously, and it was referred back to the committee for execution.

The installation of the Earl De Grey and Ripon as the Grand Master of the English Masons will take place on the 14th inst., at the Freemasons' Hall.

SUCCESFUL DIGGERS.
ON WAY FROM BENDIGO.

AUSTRALIAN GOLD DIGGINGS.

Part I.   Price 10s. 6d.

Being Twenty-Four Characteristic Sketches of Scenes, at the Iron-Bark, Bendigo, & Forest-Creek Diggings, Victoria,

TAKEN ON THE SPOT BY S. T. G.

THE interes evinced by the Public at the present time in connexion with the recently dis-covered God Fields of Australia, for which thousands of our countrymen have left their native shores, anxously hoping to share the Golden Treasures so abundantly scattered over that extensive Continent has induced the Publisher of these Sketches to lay them before the public, with the assurance that their accuracy and character will not fail to interest many of those who, from the fact of having friends and connexions engaged in the very localities and labours here depicted, will be aided by this effort to realize to their minds' eye, more vividly than otherwise could be done, the scenes, characters, and circumstances among which they are thrown.

LONDON:

Published by H. H. COLLINS & Co., 11, Great Winchester-Street, City; and PIPER BROTHERS, & Co., 23, Paternoster-Row.

1853.

H. H. COLLINS & Co., Engravers, Lithographers, Printers, and General Stationers. Bank Notes, Letters of Credit, Coupons, Shares, Certificates, Card Plates, Arms, Seals, Bankers' Cheques, Labels, Show Cards, Pattern Books, &c., Printed with care and dispatch on the Premises.

DRAWINGS AND DESIGNS MADE.

LETTER-PRESS, COPPER-PLATE, AND LITHOGRAPHIC PRINTING IN ALL THEIR VARIOUS DEPARTMENTS ON THE LOWEST POSSIBLE TERMS,

Shares, Cheques, and other Documents, consecutively Numbered by Machinery.

A series of sketches from 1853 depicting life on the Australian goldfields.

The advertisement eloquently (if with several spelling mistakes) illustrates the desire of publishers to direct 'the mind's eye' of the British people. In this case, they are being invited to view the activities of kinsmen who had emigrated to Australia. The artist is Samuel Thomas Gill. Notice the desire to emphasize authenticity in a pre-photographic age with each illustration marked 'sketched on the spot'.

JJ Empire & Colonies Box 1

WAYFARING DIGGERS.

CRADLING. FORREST CREEK.

DIGGERS HUT, FOREST CREEK.

AUSTRALIAN LIFE, ROAD TO THE DIGGINGS.

AUSTRALIAN LIFE, MOUNT ALEXANDER.

AUSTRALIAN LIFE, ARRIVAL AT SYDNEY.

Australian life (1853).

Four superb images of early colonial life in Australia, showing exotic scenes in vibrant colour (Reed & Co., London).

JJ Empire & Colonies Box 1

AUSTRALIAN LIFE, A KANGAROO HUNT.

'Original Sketches in Pen and Ink of Life and Scenes in the Colonies: South Africa – Round about Cape Town', 4 August 1877.

This supplement was published by S.W. Silver & Co. at the offices of the *Colonies and India*, 66–67 Cornhill, London. Illustrations include a view of the iconic Table Mountain, street scenes from Cape Town, and depictions of Malay women and other local peoples. The 'Cape Malay' community, a distinctive element of South Africa's population, originated during the period of Dutch rule (ended by the British when they took the Cape during the Revolutionary and Napoleonic Wars). The Dutch East India Company had imported slaves from its territories in modern-day Indonesia, particularly from Java. Others arrived as deported political dissidents.

JJ Empire & Colonies Box 1

BYWAYS OF NEW ZEALAND

IN TWO PARTS.—PART I.

WHEREABOUTS IS NEW ZEALAND? An absurd question, indeed? Everybody knows that it's at the Antipodes—right under our feet.

But how many really picture it to themselves as being "down below?" To the majority the question as to the whereabouts of New Zealand only brings back unpleasant memories of dry geography lessons, a school atlas, and a sort of horizontal figure of eight, labelled "The World." And right down, in the bottom left-hand corner, are two out-of-the-way-looking islands, that seem like big bullies driven out of the society of the innumerable little dots that swarm in the watery wastes of the South Pacific. It certainly appears, from that sort of map, as if you would have to go west to get to New Zealand.

On the other hand, people who are familiar

SELECTOR'S HUT NEAR LAKE WAKATIPU, SOUTH ISLAND

with that equally deluding picture, called "Mercator's Projection," will probably think of New Zealand as being away out in the right-hand corner of the world, and to them it would seem as if you ought to go east to get there.

At present the latter is certainly the most usual route; and a jolly voyage it is, too, if you can only afford the time to take a sailing vessel right round the Cape to Australia. It is best not to take a sailing vessel direct to New Zealand, as there are comparatively so few good direct vessels; and, besides that, it is better to see Australia before New Zealand, as the somewhat tame scenery and vegetation of the former do not show to advantage after you have been revelling in the appearance of perpetual summer in the wonderful evergreen forests of the latter. It is one of the great charms of this country that it does not much matter at what time of year you visit it. For the South Island, perhaps the best time is March or April, because then you can spend the wintry months of May and June in the warm North Island. This last sentence seems full of contradictory terms; but you soon get used to such a reversal of preconceived notions in a country where a southern aspect is the cool and shady aspect, and even the bottle has to be passed from left to right if you want to conform to old-fashioned prejudices, and make it circulate "the same way as the sun."

It is not a country to be rushed through, though you may see a good deal of it by taking one of those wonderfully cheap tickets issued by the Union Steamship Company. You can make the round from Melbourne to Sydney, touching at most of the principal ports of New Zealand, and yet the whole voyage, lasting nearly three weeks, costs only about 18*l.*, all meals included. You can stop at any port, and continue the voyage by any steamer; it was this "fatal facility" for stopping that made me linger three or four months on a visit that I had only expected to occupy so many weeks. It is so much pleasanter to be quite unfettered as to time. One of the chief drawbacks to ordinary travelling is that you have to make so many definite arrangements a long while beforehand, and that you find yourself carried about like a railway parcel right away to the destination you are labelled for. There are not many countries that have that glorious American institution of "unlimited first-class," and recognise the validity of the unused portion of your ticket as long as you live, or even longer, If your heirs like to sell it to a "scalper." It's rather a queer notion, by the by, that of the purchasing dead men's tickets in a second-hand railroad office. I wonder if the market price goes down much after a bad accident.

MINER'S CAMP, THE "INVINCIBLE" GOLD REEF, NEAR LAKE WAKATIPU

But to return to New Zealand. The four or five days' voyage from Melbourne is generally uninteresting, and almost always

NELSON, OTHERWISE CALLED "SLEEPY HOLLOW," SOUTH ISLAND

WANTED,

By a Gentlemen settled near Philadelphia, in North America,

Some Tradesmen, such as

BRICKlayers, Carpenters, Joiners, Sawyers, Stone-masons, Tilers, Slaters, Plaisterers, Surgeons, School-masters, Book-keepers, Hair-dressers, Wheel and Mill-wrights, Coopers, Black White and Copper-smiths, Linen-weavers, Shoe-makers, Taylors, Gardeners, and those of no Trade, likewise a Number of Farmers who understand the Country Business. Those who are willing to engage are desir'd to apply at No. 5, Cook's-Court, Cammomile-street, near Bishopsgate: or to Mr. *Thomas Miller*, at the City of Bristol, Irongate, near the Tower. Observe these Bills at the Window. No Apprentices will be taken, without the Consent of their Friends and Masters. The Ship will sail with all Expedition.

Merchants and Captains may be spoke with at the above Office every Day, Sundays excepted. Any Tradesmen or others, that are inclinable to go abroad, will meet with great Encouragement by applying at the above Office. Some Boys wanted, from 12 Years old to 14, 16, 18 or upwards,

A newspaper advertisement for a gentleman in Philadelphia seeking to recruit British workmen through agents in Bristol and London (*c.*1800).

It indicates the extent to which the settler colonies – even, in America's case, in the decades immediately following independence – relied upon British resources for their development.

JJ Emigration Box 1

An advertisement for land in Canada to attract settlers, from *The British News of Canada* (1911).

JJ Emigration Box 1

34

Many Homesteads Available Along Canadian Northern.

Four Million Acres of Arable Land Open for Settlement on Company's Branches.

THERE are **4,000,000** acres of free land available to settlers who locate this year near the lines of the Canadian Northern. This land is not scattered, but is in five districts. None of it is more than 30 miles from the line, and although the roads included are not all complete, they are under way, the grade being already built. All this land has been carefully gone over by representatives of the Canadian Northern, and the officials of the immigration department of the line will direct travellers to it. It is expected that thousands of the available homesteads will be taken up during the coming summer. This valuable heritage will no doubt fall into the possession of British immigrants. Much of the country included in the 4,000,000 acres tracts is such as British settlers prefer, being adapted to mixed farming, with good water and timber.

In the Battleford land district there are **3,000** homesteads available; in the Prince Albert **4,500**; in the Calgary **4,500**; and in the Edmonton **9,000**. The land referred to in the Prince Albert land district is located east of the city, chiefly between the railway line and Saskatchewan River. West of Prince Albert are **1,500** homesteads available along the route of the Crooked Lake Branch, now under construction. North-west from Battleford there are **3,000** homesteads north of the line to Athabaska Landing. They are served by the Jack Fish Lake Line. North of Edmonton there are **9,000** homesteads within reasonable distance of the line to Athabaska Landing. The grading on the line is now completed to the river. The most strategic of the new lines of the Canadian Northern is that which is now being pushed into Calgary, since it will give access to that city. Near this line in Saskatchewan and Alberta there are from **4,500**

READ THIS

IT MEANS
YOUR OPPORTUNITY

Four Million Acres of Good arable land are to be given away this year near the lines of the Canadian Northern Railway in Western Canada.

FOUR MILLION ACRES OF FREE FARMS
all near the railway.

This news item was printed in the Winnipeg *Free Press* of March 11th, 1911. Read it—and if you want a home of your own, with 160 acres of the best land on earth—all for nothing—act at once. The Canadian Northern Railway runs through the richest sections of Western Canada; OVER SIX HUNDRED MILES OF NEW LINE will be built this year. There will never be a better opportunity for you to become independent and prosperous. The only remaining free homesteads are in the territories through which the new lines of railway are being built. Thousands of land-hungry settlers are pouring in ahead of the steel.

NOW is the TIME for YOU to seize YOUR opportunity.

Write for information to :

FRED J. MOSS,
European Emigration Agent.
Craig's Court House, 21, Charing Cross,
London, S.W.

For Ex-Service Men:
Under One Flag **(1914).**

A brochure offering advice for
the would-be migrant. Canada,
represented by a farmer, tempts
British soldiers and sailors to
consider starting new lives as
settlers. In the previous year,
389,394 people had left Britain
to start new lives abroad. During
and after the First World War
there was a concerted drive to
encourage ex-servicemen and
their families to settle overseas.
Between 1815 and 1914 over
16 million people left Britain,
transforming the world in the
process. This migration hugely
expanded the numbers and size
of white settler societies overseas
and permanently changed the
economic, political and cultural
geography of the world.

JJ Military & Naval Pageants Box

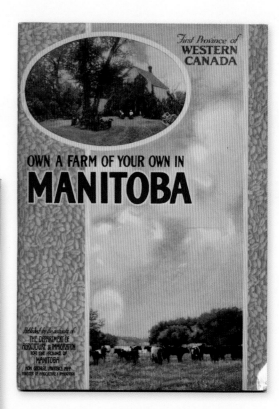

A selection of attractive brochures from the interwar period, tempting Britons to start new lives in Australia, Canada and Southern Rhodesia.

The Minister of Agriculture and Immigration in Manitoba and the Minister of Immigration and Colonization in Ottawa (1925) issued the Canadian publications, demonstrating the manner in which emigration was officially encouraged.

JJ Emigration Boxes 2 and 3

37

THE HORRORS
OF
EMIGRATION!

Or what the Eye cannot see
The Heart never grieves at.

The Miseries, Privations, and Dangers
ENDURED IN A STRANGE COUNTRY,
Away from Home, away from your Friends, Starvation and Death
does its ravages unknown to to those at home ;
and hundreds who go in the full hope of making a fortune are
NEVER AGAIN HEARD OF !

MURDERS, CRUEL TORTURES,
And Robberies by the Natives,
Whose taste for HUMAN FLESH succeeds the Horrid Deed !
The wild Poisonous Serpents and other Animals, whose Prey,
the Emigrants only, satisfying their keener appetites.
FEARFUL SHIPWRECKS from the boisterous Winds, Seas, and

ROTTEN SHIPS.

EXPOSURE OF AGENTS,
WHO WILL GET YOU TRANSPORTED TO THE
LANDS OF
Fatal Diseases, Dangerous Animals,
and Swarms of Vermin.

PUBLISHED BY WINN, HOLYWELL ST. STRAND
May be had of Cleave, Shoe Lane ; Purkiss, Compton St, Soho ; and Caffyn, Mile End.

'The Horrors of Emigration!'
(early nineteenth century).

This tract decries emigration by warning would-be
emigrants of the dangers of travelling on rotten
ships, and of the horrors of life in the new colonies
of settlement. If they made landfall the other side,
the hapless emigrants risked starvation, disease,
the predations of wild animals and wicked people,
including cannibals. Ultimately, emigration
probably meant death. The illustration shows a
settler stalked by a wild beast and with a serpent
entwined about his leg.

JJ Emigration Box 1

PROBABLE EFFECTS of OVER FEMALE-EMIGRATION, or

'Probable Effects of Over Female Emigration' (1853).

A fascinating caricature casting a satirical eye on emigration, a phenomenon that in the artist's opinion might have created the need to import women from Africa or the West Indies. Through grotesquely exaggerated caricature it purports to depict the 'Probable Effects of Over Female Emigration, or *Importing* the Fair Sex from the Savage Islands in Consequence of *Exporting* all our own to Australia!!!!!' Men gather round to inspect a group of women just off the boat, whilst in the background Redcoats rush from the fort to have a look too. The artist was George Cruikshank (1792–1878) and the image comes from his 1853 *Comic Almanack*, published by David Bogue of London. Regarded as the 'modern Hogarth', Cruikshank was well known for his political and satirical illustrations, and for his collaborative ventures with his friend Charles Dickens.

JJ Emigration Folder

§ the Fair Sex from the Savage Islands in Consequence of Exporting all our own to Australia !!!!!

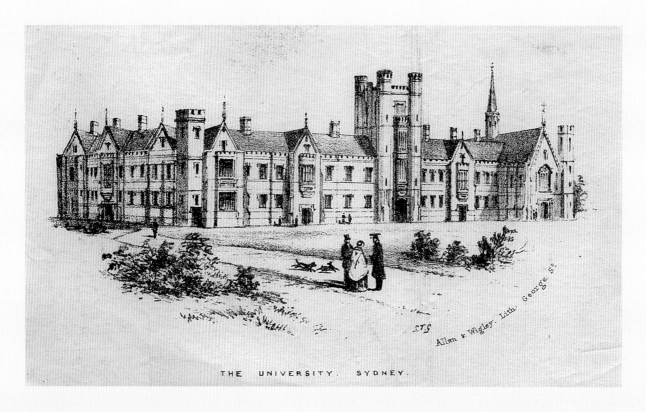

THE UNIVERSITY. SYDNEY.

The University, Sydney (*c.* 1856).

This nineteenth-century lithograph of the University of Sydney illustrates the manner in which English institutions and architectural styles were transplanted to distant parts of the world. This could be any number of Oxbridge colleges or British public schools, with its entrance tower, chapel and quadrangle featuring teaching rooms, accommodation and dining hall. The 'quad' was adorned by cloisters and jacaranda trees. Like countless other institutions around the world, it was deliberately modelled on British institutions, a fact embedded in the University's motto, *Sidere mens eadem mutato*, which means that the traditions of the universities in the northern hemisphere are continued in those of the southern hemisphere. The artist, Samuel Thomas Gill (1818–1880), was an emigrant from Britain who produced several lithographs in 1856 that were published as *In and Around Sydney*. Born in Somerset, he emigrated to South Australia with his parents in 1839. In the early 1840s he was a draftsman on an expedition to the Spencer Gulf. He named Lake Gill (now Lake Dutton) and subsequently raffled his pictures from the expedition. In 1852 he tried his hand on the Victorian gold diggings.

JJ Empire & Colonies Box 3

W.H.Bartlett. J.H.Lekeux.

Interior of the Cathedral, Montreal (nineteenth century).

An example of the way in which European architecture and traditions were transplanted to the colonies. J.H. Lekeux's steel engraving (after W.H. Bartlett) depicts the gothic revival interior of Montreal's nineteenth-century Notre Dame Cathedral.

JJ Empire & Colonies Box 1

The 'welcome given in Melbourne, Australia to a primrose from England'.

This rather unusual lithograph is from the *Illustrated London News* of 16 October 1858. A primrose had been taken to Australia in a Wardian case and upwards of three thousand people came to see it. The news led Edward Hopley (1816–1869) to paint a picture, which was exhibited at the Royal Academy in 1855. 'A primrose had been taken to Australia in a covered glass case, and when it arrived there in full bloom, the sensation it excited as a reminiscence of "fatherland" was so great, that it was necessary to protect it with a guard.' It is an example of Victorian sentimentality, and captures the sense of isolation experienced by early settlers cut off from the land of their birth.

JJ Emigration Folder

CHRISTMAS GIFTS FOR FRIENDS ABROAD

Members are notified that as the Christmas List, containing the latest Novelties, will not be published before the middle of November and will therefore be too late for those wishing to send presents overseas, this special list is issued now to enable Members to select suitable Xmas gifts for their friends abroad. The late.t dates for posting parcels to the undermentioned countries are :—

AUSTRALIA	South Victoria and New South Wales	November 1st
	West	November 9th
	Queensland and Tasmania	November 1st
CANADA	Western	November 30th
	Eastern	December 7th
CHINA		October 25th
EAST AFRICA		November 8th
EGYPT		November 29th
INDIA		November 15th
JAPAN		October 25th
NEW ZEALAND		November 2nd
SOUTH AFRICA		November 23rd
RHODESIA via Cape Town		November 23rd
U.S.A.	Western	December 5th
	Eastern	December 12th

Seen on the Front Cover

F.R.4158. Snakeskin, lined art. silk, divided inner compartment and mirror. Size 8 × 5¼ ins. deep. Colours : fawn, red, blue and green. (British.)
Price 21/-

F.R.4113. Morocco Zip-opening Bag, assorted colours, lined moiré poplin, fitted double frame and mirror. Size 10¾ × 7 ins. (British.)
Price 10/6

F.R.4168. Morocco Bag, size 9½ × 6 ins. deep, lined art. silk with divided inner compartment and mirror in pocket. Assorted colours.
Price 15/-

F.R.4159. Useful Bag with chromium-plated mount, lined art. silk, with divided inner compartment and mirror. Size 11 × 6½ ins. deep. (British.)
Covered Morocco Leather. Colours : grey, blue, brown and black 21/-
Covered Fine Seal Leather (black). 29/6
Ditto, in colours to order 34/-

F.R.4167. Lizard-skin Bag, lined art. silk, size 8 × 6 ins. deep, with divided inner compartment and mirror in pocket. (British.)
Price 21/-

Fitted Bag Department
Army & Navy Stores, Westminster, S.W.1
1

Army & Navy Co-operative Society, Ltd, stores circular (1933).

A department store catalogue from October 1933 showing an advertisement for Christmas gifts for friends abroad that strikes a classic colonial pose.

JJ Women's Clothes and Millinery 8 (24)

The British Emigrant (1907).

An example of the kind of publication called into existence by the buoyancy of emigration, this is the first volume of the weekly journal *The British Emigrant* (May 1907). Its cover illustrates some of the preoccupations of the settler, such as finding a removal company that specialized in overseas relocation, the need to be able to send parcels to and from the colonies, the benefit of travel insurance, and the offer to emigrants of free or assisted passage from colonial governments seeking to increase their white population and develop their skilled labour force. The inclusion of an article on the 'Matrimonial Bureau for Colonists' and of an advert for a private detective agency specializing in divorce and commercial investigations indicate some of factors involved in (or potentially resulting from) emigration; whilst some men were leaving unwanted families behind, others were making off with ill-gotten gains. Behind the title can be seen a classic imperial design construction; a nonchalant British lion presiding over the globe, an Australian black swan, the thistle and shamrock of Scotland and Ireland respectively, and a nautical device.

JJ Emigration Box 1

The 1913 annual report of the British Women's Emigration Association, founded in 1901.

According to the Women's Library, initiatives to 'encourage educated middle class women to emigrate in an effort to relieve the pressures of population growth and the perceived problem of the number of "superfluous" unmarried women, led to the foundation of several organizations'. In 1884, former members of the Women's Emigration Society formed the United Englishwoman's Emigration Register, which went on to become the United Englishwoman's Emigration Association. Its aims were to 'emigrate women of good character, to ensure their safety during and after their travel and to keep in touch with them for some time after their arrival. By 1888, the group began to work

in co-operation with the Scotch Girl's Friendly Association and the Scottish YWCA, prompting a change of name. The following year the new United British Women's Emigration Association changed the original constitution, centralizing what had been a loose grouping of independent workers and outlining their responsibilities, roles and relationships. Their expansion continued, from the establishment of Irish and Scottish branches in 1889 to one in Staffordshire and one for Wiltshire and Somerset that same year, while another was established in Bath in 1891. Homes for emigrants waiting to depart were created in Liverpool in 1887 and in London in 1893. The majority of emigrants which passed through them in the 1890s were destined for Canada, New Zealand or Australia, but towards the end of the century, the flow of emigrants to South Africa increased to such a degree that it became necessary to set up a South African Expansion Scheme Committee. This would go on to become the independent South African Colonization Society. In 1901, the parent organization dropped the "united" element of its name and continued to expand in their own fields, opening a hostel at Kelowna in British Colombia in 1913. After the outbreak of the First World War the number of emigrants declined. In 1917, a Joint Council of Women's Emigration Societies was established to deal with the situation after the war and liaise with central government. This co-operation between the British Women's Emigration Association, the Colonial Intelligence League and the South African Colonization Society finally resulted in their amalgamation into the Society for the Overseas Settlement of British Women in Dec 1919.' (*The Women's Library: Records of the British Women's Emigration Association*).

JJ Emigration Box 1

President : THE COUNTESS OF DUDLEY.
Hon. President : THE HON. MRS. JOYCE.

THE IMPERIAL INSTITUTE.

For information and advice apply to
MISS LEFROY, Hon. Sec.,
Office of the British Women's Emigration Association,
Imperial Institute, London, S.W.

The Imperial Colonist (1902).

This is another publication given life by the volume of emigration from Britain to the settler colonies. It was the organ of the British Women's Emigration Association. One of its key objectives was to ensure *protected* emigration – to see that only people (particularly women) of 'good character' emigrated, and that they were looked after whilst at sea and upon arrival. There is a clear moral undertone. In Britain, people such as Edward Gibbon Wakefield drew up plans for the creation of 'model' colonies in which the social balance between classes was perfectly replicated, and the 'right type' of people were selected. The magazine carried adverts for the Union Castle Shipping Line and its Royal Mail Services to South and East Africa.

JJ Emigration Box 1

The Colonial Training Home for Girls at Leaton, Wrockwardine, in Wellington, Shropshire (early twentieth century).

The Home specialized in preparing girls for domestic service in the settler colonies. 'Washing and ironing, dairy-work, the care of poultry, cooking, sewing, and dress-making are taught.' Many children from the workhouses were adopted by Canadian foster parents, according to Marjorie Kohli, 'and are being sent out by the United British Women's Emigration Association', with which this training establishment had strong connections. (Marjorie Kohli, *The Golden Bridge: Young Emigrants to Canada, 1833–1939*).

JJ Emigration Box 1

***The Imperial and Colonial Magazine
and Review* of 1 November 1900,
edited by E.F. Benson and 'Celt'.**

Its slogan was *Imperium et Libertas*, which was a
popular phrase at the time bandied about by, among
others, the young Winston Churchill as he changed
career from soldier to politician. A phrase that
today appears paradoxical – how can empire stand
alongside liberty? – it reflected a common view of
the beneficence of British rule and its compatibility
with progress and freedom. According to this line
of thinking, liberty was the freedom to get on with
daily life in a well-ordered society, where the rule
of law pertained and rulers were just and fair. The
British, they were fond of thinking, provided this
kind of rule, and freedom followed.

JJ Prospectuses of Journals 30 (16)

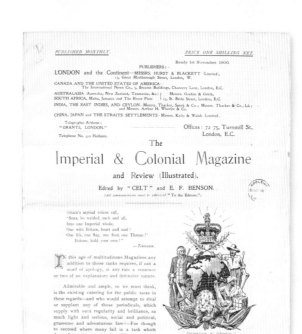

Britannia (*c.* 1900).

The magazine for closer union between the home
country and the colonies, with an engraving by
Joseph Swain (1820-1909), showing Britannia on a
map of the world. This magazine was the organ of
the National Unity Movement.

JJ Prospectuses of Journals 8 (30)

IMPERIAL AUTHORITY:
CIVIC AND MILITARY

This chapter considers ephemera associated with the political and administrative structures that governed the British Empire. At the apex sat the monarch; beneath that, offices of state in Whitehall and dominion prime ministers, as well as governors, viceroys and consuls-general. Beneath this tier came the provincial and district commissioners, and finally the indigenous princes, chiefs and sub-chiefs. The monarchy was increasingly imperialized during the reigns of Victoria and her successors. The commemoration of coronations, jubilees and royal weddings occurred not just in Britain but throughout the Empire, including in non-white sectors that were heavily anglicized, such as the West Indies. Empire Day and royal occasions provided an opportunity for colonial authorities to deploy the rhetoric of imperial benevolence and to impress the locals with fireworks, marching bands and garden parties. What the locals made of it all, of course, differed widely. Some were duly impressed, some indifferent, some contemptuous of British pretensions and the inequity of rule by foreign intruders. Nevertheless, the British enjoyed considerable success in co-opting indigenous elites to share in the enterprise of ruling an enormous and diverse empire.

In addition to the ubiquitous image of the imperial monarch, found in public buildings and on coins and postage stamps in every territory of the Empire, there were the representatives of British authority in the flesh. The image of the British colonial administrator, complete with pith helmet or white tropical kit, was well known to the British public, as was the image of the indigenous ruler, most commonly in the form of the Indian maharajah or the African chief. Imperial authority was also manifest in the form of British and indigenously recruited military and police forces. All of these aspects of imperial authority created ephemera in the form of advertisements, pictures, official forms and memorabilia.

As the political power of the monarchy declined, its ceremonial and symbolic role increased. This was expressed through the involvement of dominions and colonies with imperial events held in Britain, such as the 1907 colonial conference with its attendant banquets, and tours by kings and princes overseas. Victoria opened the Indian and Colonial Exhibition of 1886 and laid the foundation stone for the Imperial Institute in a ceremony steeped in imperial pageantry. Though Victoria managed a state visit to Ireland, royal tours of the Empire began in earnest during the reign of Edward VII and were continued by all of his successors.

In India and elsewhere the British adopted the princely practice of holding durbars, public audiences and official receptions given by monarchs, viceroys and governors ('durbar' comes from the Urdu *darbār*, meaning court). The Delhi Durbar of 1911 was a groundbreaking event that took the King and Queen physically to India to be crowned Emperor and Empress of that land. The 1911 Durbar site covered twenty-five square miles, and its vast canvas-covered camps were connected by sixty miles of new road and thirty miles of railway. During his Indian tour of the 1870s, the Prince of

49

Wales held durbars for indigenous princes, went tiger shooting and travelled with his entourage on howdah-bearing state elephants marked with the Prince's fleur-de-lys crest. Touring monarchs and princes participated in the parliamentary life of imperial territories, laying foundation stones, disbursing gifts such as dispatch boxes and maces modelled on those of the British parliament, and attending state openings.

During the reign of Victoria the monarchy had become very publicly associated with empire as the Queen was transformed from 'petulant widow to imperial matriarch'.[1] Victoria's golden and diamond jubilees were internationally choreographed festivals of imperial symbolism, as was her funeral. During her long reign Victoria had become a potent national symbol, her dour profile displayed in classrooms and government offices all over the world. From Canada Winston Churchill wrote to his mother: 'So the Queen is dead. The news reached us at Winnipeg and this city far away among the snows – fourteen hundred miles from any British town of importance – began to hang its head and hoist half-masted flags. A great and solemn event.'[2]

A day of mourning was proclaimed throughout the Empire. Illustrating the manner in which the monarchy was portrayed as an omniscient institution still carrying vestiges of the semi-divine, as soon as his mother had passed away Edward VII issued a statement 'to my people beyond the seas'. This colourful item emphasized the monarchy's association with the Empire, as well as the continuity in world affairs that Britain stood for, the familial concept of the British world community, and the solicitousness of a caring and benevolent ruler. Half a century later, Elizabeth II's coronation in 1953 was seized upon as an opportunity to reaffirm Britain's place in an increasingly troubled world. A new 'Elizabethan age' was proclaimed and the event was wrapped in imperial imagery and language, from the coronation procession itself to New Zealander Edmund Hillary's fortuitous conquest of Everest at the same time.[3]

Beneath the monarch in the pyramid of imperial authority, but exercising the real political power, stood the imperial parliament at Westminster and the Whitehall offices of state. There were secretaries of state for the colonies, the dominions and India. The dominions' prime ministers, and the high commissioners who represented them overseas, were also part of the Empire's system of governance. A good deal of business was conducted by Britain and the dominions through the innovation in 1887 of regular colonial conferences, forerunners of today's Commonwealth Heads of Government Meetings.

In addition to these almost exclusively 'white' elements of empire and imperial governance, there was a dense network of non-European authorities with whom and through whom the British administered the non-white territories. Without them British rule would not have been practicable, given that the British were never going to invest the amount of blood and treasure necessary to directly rule an alien population of nearly half a billion people. Many parts of the Empire were lightly ruled from the centre, and so indigenous rulers held on to real power. Ruling elites included the rulers of India's 350-plus princely states and the chiefs, emirs, kings, sheikhs and sultans of Britain's disparate colonies and associated territories. Indigenous political authorities also remained significant in the settler colonies, although European expansion had done much to erode the strength of indigenous polities through conquest, land alienation and the ravages of disease. Nevertheless, the power of the Maori chiefs remained a factor in New Zealand's 'internal settlement' following the Maori wars; in South Africa, though much reduced, the authority of the Zulu royal house remained extant; and a Royal Proclamation of 1763 confirmed the role in Canadian politics of what would later be termed the 'First Nations'.

Indigenous political leaders operated in conjunction with that enduring symbol of British authority, the district officer. The district officer (or district commissioner, or resident, or collector, according to the region of the Empire in which he served) was part of a cadre of jack-of-all-trade administrators who were the face of British rule 'on the ground'. They were responsible for taxation, census returns, justice, public works, development projects and elections. They belonged to the Indian Civil Service, the Colonial Administrative Service and the Sudan Political Service.[4] In some parts of the Empire private companies, such as the East India Company and the British South Africa Company, were in charge.

Above the chiefs and district officers, who acted as the interface between imperial power and people 'on the ground', sat intermediaries at provincial and colony level – the governors and viceroys appointed as the sovereign's personal representative and de facto head of state in all colonial territories. In the twentieth century they were responsible for establishing and operating new political institutions, such as legislative councils, advisory boards and nascent parliaments elected on a democratic basis. British rule created local civil services and parliaments and the institutions of local government and municipal councils. As the images considered in this chapter show, even at the headwaters of the Nile, town halls and mayors' banquets were a feature of political life, though the subsequent history of these transplanted institutions has been a troubled one.

Underpinning the authority of governors, district officers and chiefs were military forces and police forces. The Gold Coast Police force, for example, comprised African constables under British officers, its symbol – a Crown surrounded by cacao leaves, cocoa beans, an elephant and a palm tree – illustrating the blend of British and indigenous elements common in the imagery relating to imperial rule and authority. Though preferably held in abeyance, military power was a vital component of imperial authority, and war and violence played a prominent role in the extension of imperial boundaries. Euphemisms such as 'pacification' and 'imperial policing' often meant death and dispossession for indigenous populations, and British rule was, ultimately, based on force and a monopoly of lethal violence. What was commonly known as 'imperial defence', meanwhile, was the British government's strategy for defending its far-flung imperial borders and the sea lanes that connected them, based on the might of the Royal Navy and the 'articles of war' which governed it. 'Gunboat diplomacy' became a synonym for the use of naval power to coerce overseas rulers. Indigenously recruited armed forces and police forces were a key feature of British rule. They formed one of the most visible aspects of empire for the British public because of their involvement in British wars, both large and small, and their appearance in London for coronations and victory parades. Whilst the Empire's military formations performed a wide range of ceremonial duties, they were all trained to fight, and the ceremonial aspects of military service were themselves important buttresses of British prestige. Images relating to imperial rule and the military formations that supported it encouraged the glorification of war discernible from late Victorian times, as wars – particularly colonial wars – came to be seen as 'theatrical events of sombre magnificence'.[5]

A commemorative souvenir for the Golden Jubilee of Victoria (1887).

The 1887 Jubilee marked not only the longevity of Victoria's reign, but the imperialization of the monarchy that had taken place since her accession to the throne in 1837, and this stylized souvenir – complete with ornamental border and showing the titles 'Queen of Great Britain' and 'Empress of India' – marked the occasion. The Jubilee also marked the extent to which the Empire had grown in that period, and the sense of imperial fervour that had gripped the British public – or at least some sections of it – by the 1880s. The jubilee spawned a huge range of commemorative material, from florins and stamps to tableware, posters and statues, a fact indicated today by the volume of activity in the antiques market. Composers composed and poets rhapsodized, parish committees and town councils planned civic events and built ceremonial arches, and dominions' governments devised showy ways in which to mark the occasion at home whilst simultaneously participating in the mother country's celebrations. It was a truly global moment, in which almost every hamlet, village, town and city throughout the Empire held public commemorations – parties, pageants, parades, church services, and the lighting of beacons from hill to hill, as Housman's poem recorded. In London there was a banquet for over fifty heads of state, a service at Westminster Abbey, and a huge procession featuring soldiery drawn from all over the Empire. Not everyone in the Empire had the same idea about how the Jubilee should be celebrated, however, and Irish republicans plotted to assassinate the Queen during the Westminster Abbey service.

JJ Ceremonial Box 3

QUEEN OF GREAT BRITAIN.

1887.

JUBILEE

YEAR.

Queen Victoria

Born
May 24th, 1819.
Accession
June 20th, 1837.

EMPRESS OF INDIA.

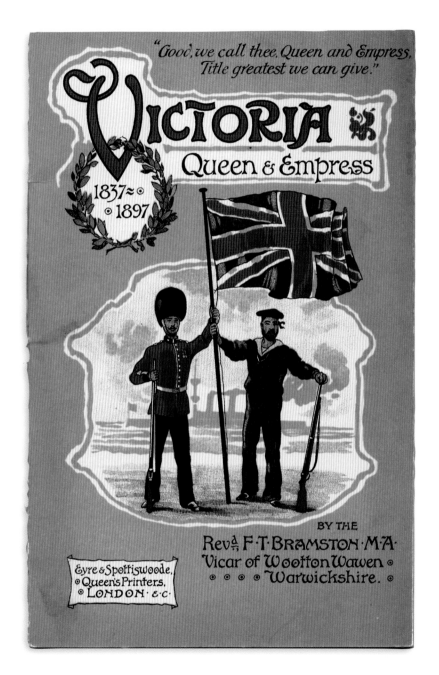

"Good, we call thee, Queen and Empress, Title greatest we can give."

VICTORIA
Queen & Empress
1837 ~ 1897

BY THE
Revᵈ F·T·BRAMSTON·M·A·
Vicar of Wootton Wawen
Warwickshire.

Eyre & Spottiswoode,
Queen's Printers,
LONDON·E·C·

Victoria Queen and Empress: front cover of a poem by the Reverend F.T. Bramston (1897).

A typically patriotic piece of Jubilee memorabilia. The picture shows a guardsman (representing the Army) and a matelot (representing the Navy), with a battleship steaming in the background. The 1897 Diamond Jubilee, like its 1887 predecessor, was a major national and imperial event marked by celebrations across the world, centred on a lavish London jamboree. In this publication, the Reverend F.T. Bramston praises the Queen's goodness and the achievements of her reign through poetry, a familiar form of Victorian hagiography. The Queen was eulogized along with national heroes such as Nelson and Gordon. The length of her reign, and the reinvention of the monarchy that occurred during it, had made her a symbol of the nation above criticism or contempt. Reverend Bramston's poem was not very good.

JJ Ceremonial Box 3

**The Royal Visit to Uganda:
a commemorative souvenir
brochure (1954).**

The Queen visited Uganda as
part of her post-coronation
imperial tour.

JJ Empire & Colonies Box 4

Souvenir programme for a Royal Albert Hall Banquet held in honour of the dominion prime ministers (1907).

The dominion prime ministers had gathered in London to attend the 1907 colonial conference (15 April to 14 May). At this conference it was decided that in future the name of the gathering would be changed to 'Imperial Conference' (as opposed to 'Colonial Conference'), and that they would be held at regular intervals rather than in the ad hoc manner in which they had convened since their inception at the time of the 1887 Jubilee. The change in name reflected the fact that the dominions were no longer colonies, in that they were substantially self-governing and party to decision-making at the imperial centre in London – whereas colonies were directly ruled by British governors and had no voice in the councils of the imperial metropole. As the dominions grew in political maturity they demanded increasing access to imperial decision-making, particularly with regard to imperial defence policy in their own regions. The colonial conferences became the major means of giving substance to these wishes. As under-secretary of state at the Colonial Office, Winston Churchill was heavily involved in hosting the 1907 conference, the sixth since 1887. The border of the title page (*right*) shows the names of many British possessions; the second illustration (*right, top*) reproduces a Rudyard Kipling poem that captured the rhetoric of shared interest that was common in discussions of Britain and the settler colonies, soon to be written in blood during the First World War. The third image (*right, bottom*) shows a vigorous Britannia defending Britain's shores, an arresting illustration by Bernard Partridge (1861–1945).

JJ Empire & Colonies Box 2

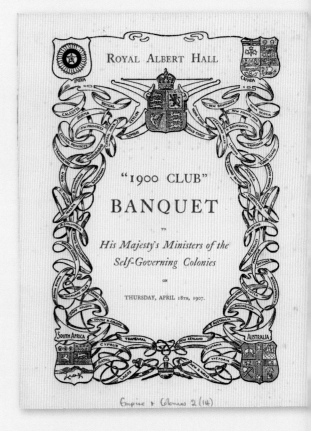

The Song of the English

From the " Seven Seas "

By Rudyard Kipling.

Also, we will make promise. So long as The Blood
endures,

I shall know that your good is mine: ye shall feel that
my strength is yours:

In the day of Armageddon, at the last great fight of all,

That our House stand together and the pillars do not fall.

Draw not the threefold knot firm on the ninefold bands,

And the Law that ye make shall be law after the rule of
your lands.

This for the Waxen Heath, and that for the Wattle-bloom

This for the Maple Leaf, and that for the Southern Broom.

The Law that ye make shall be law, and I do not press
my will,

Because ye are Sons of the Blood and call me Mother still.

4

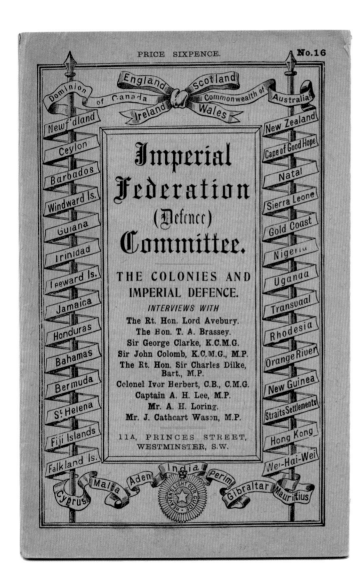

**The Colonies and Imperial Defence,
an Imperial Federation (Defence)
Committee pamphlet (1900s).**

Note the names of numerous British possessions on
either side of the text. The Committee was part of
the Imperial Federation League, founded in 1884.
Lord Rosebery was the first president of the British
branch. The League believed that the federation
of the Empire was absolutely vital to its survival
and advocated the establishment of a genuine
Imperial Parliament. The League was instrumental
in organizing the first colonial conference, which
brought together colonial prime ministers in
London for the 1887 jubilee celebrations. Among
other things, the League campaigned for a more
equitable division of the burden of defending the
Empire; specifically, it believed that the white
dominions contributed too little to imperial defence,
whilst the British taxpayer contributed far too much.
As the pamphlet makes clear, whilst one-fifth of
the Empire's trade belonged to the colonies, they
contributed less than one-hundredth of the cost of
its protection. The League also acted as a rallying
point for 'race patriots', people who espoused the
need for those of British blood to multiply and
settle around the world. Merging with this trend,
and contributing to what has become known as
'social imperialism', in the late nineteenth and early
twentieth centuries it became common to associate
racial vigour and national and imperial survival
with improved health provisions at home.

JJ Empire & Colonies Box 1

**Mungha-Kau, Chief of
Roto-aire Lake, with
Ko-mari, his wife (1846).**

An illustration from the *Pictorial
Review* depicting a Maori chief
and his wife.

JJ Empire & Colonies Folder

**A nobleman in Ceylon
(late eighteenth century).**

This image is of a nobleman, emphasizing the status of indigenous elites within the imperial system. Its provenance is uncertain, despite the best efforts of experts from the British Museum, the Victoria & Albert Museum, the Courtauld Institute of Art, and Oxford and Cambridge Universities. He is dressed in an eighteenth-century-style military coat with frogging, and his dhoti, with kastane with lion-headed hilt, is almost certainly one of the distinctive types produced on the Coromandel coast for export to Ceylon. He has a bronze oval tobacco container slung on a chain across his chest. These facts, an expert at the British Museum concludes, all point to the image being of Ceylon in the late eighteenth century, when Ceylon was ruled by the Dutch.

JJ Empire & Colonies Folder

Transport of the Raj (*c.* 1870).

A caparisoned elephant – bearing a coronet and fleur-de-lys, quite possibly representing the Prince of Wales's tour in the mid-1870s. Elephants were potent symbols of rule and power, for Indian rulers as well as their British successors. Coats of arms and badges, such as those for the colony of Ceylon, for Persia and Iraq Command, and for the 18th (Indian) Division, often featured elephants. Before conservation became fashionable, many Britons valued elephants for sport, and great slaughter took place in India and Ceylon. Ivory was widely traded, elephants' feet made good umbrella stands, and their penises notable golf caddies. The explorer-settler Sir Herbert Baker killed scores of elephants in Ceylon when he settled there in the 1840s. Meanwhile, among the Hindu population of South Asia the elephant was considered sacred. Aside from sport, elephants were prized by the British for labour and for war. They were expert loggers in Burma's teak forests, and war elephants accompanied General Napier from Bombay to Abyssinia in 1868. In the Second World War elephants were vital for military clearing and construction work in the India–Burma theatre; in Ceylon and in the Cocos-Keeling Islands they were used to drag aircraft around military airstrips.

JJ Empire & Colonies Box 2

INSTRUCTIONS For the CONDUCT of the SHIPS of WAR, EXPLANATORY of, and RELATIVE to the SIGNAL-BOOK.

Instructions For the Conduct of the Ships of War (*c.* 1776–1800).

Britain's authority rested upon the warships of the Royal Navy. The Admiralty's *Signal Book for Ships of War* laid down the system of communications at sea used throughout the Revolutionary and Napoleonic Wars.

JJ Labels 22 (88a)

British forces, North West Frontier (*c.* 1880).
JJ Empire & Colonies Box 2

'The Triumphal Entry into Delhi' and 'Fall of Delhi 1857'.

Feats of arms throughout the Empire were widely celebrated and commemorated in British popular culture. Here we see John Pridham's popular 'battle march' entitled 'The Triumphal Entry into Delhi', and Stephen Glover's 'Fall of Delhi 1857', a march for the pianoforte.

JJ Music Titles 4 (66), JJ Music Titles 4 (47)

'Captain Arthur Knyvet Wilson RN engages in single combat with several Arabs' 1884. (*right*)

A typically jingoistic late Victorian image glorifying colonial warfare. This illustration of the Battle of Teb by military artist Harry Payne (1858–1927) was reproduced in the popular press and used in magic lantern displays. Images like this also appeared in magic lantern series. Wilson's VC was won during the second Battle of Teb, fought during the unsuccessful Anglo-Egyptian campaign against the Mahdi in 1884. At the start of February 1884 forces had been deployed from Suakin on the Sudanese coast in an attempt to relieve inland garrisons. General Valentine Baker led a force of 3,500 men inland, but was attacked by a force of 1,000 Sudanese commanded by Osman Digna. Baker's largely Egyptian force was inexperienced and fled, though only about 700 escaped. Predictably, British public opinion was incensed, and before the month was out General Sir Gerald Graham and a force of 4,500 men moved inland. Over 2,000 enemy soldiers were killed and Graham received the thanks of Parliament and was promoted to lieutenant general. Wilson rose to the rank of Admiral of the Fleet, and served as First Sea Lord.

JJ Scraps 6 (45a)

VICTORIA CROSS-GALLERY. CAPTAIN A.R. WILSON,
ROYAL NAVY, ENGAGING IN SINGLE COMBAT WITH SEVERAL ARABS
WITH ONLY THE HILT OF HIS SWORD, THE BLADE
HAVING BEEN BROKEN OFF.
BATTLE OF TEB
29ᵗʰ FEBRUARY 1884.

11

HARRY PAYNE

Attestation of a soldier for the Honourable East India Company's army (1767).

This man haled from Holt in Norfolk. He was nineteen years old and stood five feet seven inches in height. His illiteracy is shown by the cross as a signature. The attestation form, signed on 7 October 1767, asks the recruit to confirm that he is a Protestant and commits him to a minimum of five years' service at St Helena or any portion of the Company's Indian domains. The East India Company's armies underpinned its trading activities and were instrumental in its territorial claims and administrative activities. East India Company soldiers expanded the Company's holdings, and were used to support the wider policies of the British government, especially in times of war, as during the Seven Years War and the Napoleonic and Revolutionary Wars. In wartime, the Company's three armies (Bengal, Madras and Bombay) expanded in order to subdue Asian rivals and their European allies. Thus in 1793 the three armies numbered 18,768 European and 69,622 Indian soldiers. By 1815, the year in which the Napoleonic Wars ended, they had expanded to 31,611 Europeans and 195,572 Indians (figures from *Parliamentary Papers, 1831–32*, vol. XIII, 'Report from the Select Committee on the Affairs of the East India Company'). Even after Company rule ended in 1858 and the British Crown took over, India was Britain's 'barrack in an Oriental sea'. The Indian Army's swansong came in the imperial victories over the Japanese in India and Burma in 1944-45; its nadir – from a British point of view, at least – had come with the Sepoy Rebellion that precipitated the great Indian Mutiny of 1857-58.

JJ East India Company Box 1

UNPARALLELED SUCCESS.
The Number Printed Exceeds 1,700,000 Copies.

THE
NAVY & ARMY
ILLUSTRATED.

PUBLISHED BY
HUDSON & KEARNS, LONDON, S.E.,
AND BY GEORGE NEWNES, LTD.
10, SOUTHAMPTON STREET, W.C.

Published Fortnightly.—Price SIXPENCE.
First Issue December 20th, 1895.

OUR INDIAN CAVALRY

PRESS OPINIONS.

The Army & Navy Gazette—"Well described as 'a Magazine descriptive and illustrative of every-day life in the defensive services of the British Empire.' No such series of pictures illustrative of the Navy and the Army has ever been published. Admirable in themselves as photographs from life and from interesting events and places, the highest skill has been brought to bear in the reproductive process, and alike in paper, print and binding, the volume leaves nothing to be desired."

The Times—"'Magnificently illustrated. . . The popular magazine of the Services,' NAVY AND ARMY ILLUSTRATED, which is edited by Commander Charles N. Robinson, R.N. (Hudson & Kearns and George Newnes). We can hardly imagine an easier way of getting to learn the essential facts, not only about the uniforms of the different regiments and the build of the different ships, and not only about the features of the leading officers, but about the real life in barracks or on board a man-of-war than by studying this magazine. Almost every page contains one or two capital photographs, and the explanatory text contains all that is necessary to make them intelligible."

Telegraph—"Superbly illustrated."

P.T.O.

Front page of *The Navy & Army Illustrated* showing cavalrymen (1895).

This is the first volume of this periodical, dated 20 December 1895. Its subtitle was *A Magazine Descriptive and Illustrative of Everyday Life in the Defensive Services of the British Empire.*

JJ Prospectuses of Journals 38 (51a)

Advertisements for food products, showing imperial forces (*c.* 1890–1920).

The Indian Army was a major force in creating Britain's Asian empire, deployed across the subcontinent and beyond. Indian forces were regularly deployed for internal security and war-fighting duties in Southeast Asia, the Dutch East Indies, the Persian Gulf, East Africa and the Middle East. An entire Indian Army corps served on the Western Front during the First World War. The first illustration shows the Viceroy's bodyguard, an advertisement for cornflour from the 1890s. The second illustration shows the 10th Madras Lancers on a collectable card for Pascall's mints (*c.* 1910s–20s). The company advertised their bulls' eyes 'as supplied to the Army and Navy'. The images demonstrate the use of imperial fighting forces in the advertising of everyday products.

JJ Food 4 (16), JJ Cocoa, Chocolate and Confectionery 4 (10e)

A Nigerian Year calendar (1938).

The entry for June depicts the district officer on tour.

JJ Empire & Colonies Box 4

I THINK the June days are the best of all—
The cool soft mornings, when the sun's fierce glow
Is tempered by the clouds that, brooding low,
Turban with fleecy white the hill-tops tall.
Now will the wise man travel. Rain may fall,
Grass roofs may leak and sudden torrents flow;
The miry paths may bring sad overthrow
Of load and bearer; yet when we recall
Our journey, such brief woes come not to mind:
But we shall not forget the dimly bright
Moon-births, and how the ranges stood outlined
Against the golden sunset's fading light,
While through the ripening millet breathed a wind
That whispered to the world, " Good night, good night."

JUNE

	SUN.	•	5	12	19	26
MON.	•	6	13	20	27
TUES.	•	7	14	21	28
WED.	1	8	15	22	29
THUR.	2	9	16	23	30
FRI.	3	10	17	24	•
SAT.	4	11	18	25	•

The emblem of the Gold Coast Police force (1957).

This emblem is an excellent example of British and colonial design fusion – the Crown is surrounded by cacao leaves and cocoa beans, an elephant and a palm tree. The image shown here is taken from the force's operational orders for the 1957 independence ceremonies.

JJ Empire & Colonies Box 4

The Chairman and Members of the

Jinja Township Authority

have the pleasure to invite

to a *Civic Luncheon* given by
the Jinja Municipal Council, to be attended by
His Excellency the Governor and Lady Cohen
which will be held in the Lohana Community Hall, Jinja,
(immediately opposite the Victoria Nile School)
on Thursday, the 3rd January, 1957, at
approximately 12-30 p.m. following the
inaugural meeting of the Council

R. S. V. P.
THE TOWN CLERK
P. O. BOX 720,
JINJA,
ON OR BEFORE 19TH DECEMBER 1956.

Menu

Grapefruit Cocktail

—

Lobster Mayonnaise
or
Vegetable Cutlets

—

Chicken Pilau
or
Vegetable Curry and Rice

—

Fruit Trifle
Fruit Salad and Cream

—

Coffee

Her Majesty the Queen
Proposed by
The Chairman.

The Jinja Municipal Council
Proposed by
His Excellency the Governor,
Sir Andrew Cohen, K. C. M. G., K. C. V. O., O. B. E.
Response by
The Chairman

The Guests
Proposed by
Councillor the Hon. C. K. Patel, M. B. E.
Responses by
The Minister of Local Government
(The Hon. L. M. Boyd, C. M. G.)
and
The Worshipful the Mayor of Kampala
(Councillor C. Lewis)

The Officers of the Council
Proposed by
Councillor A. I. James
Response by
The Town Clerk.
(Mr. C. Martin, O. B. E.)

---

*Jinja Municipal
Council*

Menu

*Civic Luncheon
held on the occasion of the
Inaugural Meeting of the Council
on the
3rd January, 1957.*

Invitation and menu cards for a Civic Luncheon given by the Jinja Municipal Council (1957).

An interesting example of the growth of British municipal structures in the most unlikely parts of the world. The event is a Civic Luncheon given by the Jinja Municipal Council in the Jinja Township Authority, a European-style banquet involving familiar courses and toasts, presided over by Africans. The event was attended by His Excellency the Governor Sir Andrew Cohen and Lady Cohen. The venue was the Community Hall opposite Victoria Nile School, and marked the Council's inaugural meeting. Jinja is located in the kingdom of Buganda. The Queen had visited Jinja on her Empire Tour of 1954, but had not visited Buganda's capital, Kampala. At the time there was some hostility to the British in Buganda because of the exile of the Kabaka (king), Freddie Mutesa, in the previous year; the Cambridge-educated traditional ruler was a guest of the British taxpayer staying in a suite at the Savoy Hotel in London. He had been exiled because Buganda nationalism was hindering the development of a *Ugandan* national identity, viewed as a vital prelude to independence. Jinja offered a wonderful view of the Ripon Falls, where the Queen opened the Owen Falls Scheme, a major damming project undertaken for the generation of electricity. Churchill had visited there on his Africa tour in 1908 and dreamt of harnessing the mighty falls; after inaugurating the Owen Falls Scheme, the Queen telegrammed Prime Minister Churchill with the message 'Your vision has become reality.'

JJ Empire & Colonies Box 5

3

EXPLORATION AND KNOWLEDGE

A major cause of British engagement with the wider world was the desire to explore (leading to numerous publicly acclaimed 'discoveries'), to acquire knowledge (involving the collection of data and artefacts), and to 'improve' people of 'primitive' culture (converting them to Christianity or to 'superior' socio-economic practices). This chapter looks at ways in which the world was 'opened up' to the Western gaze, creating a plethora of images of non-Western societies in the public domain that helped shape the way that Westerners 'saw' the non-European world.

Knowledge and understanding about the Empire and the wider non-European world was generated by explorers and missionaries, as well as Army and Navy personnel, geologists, botanists, employees of private companies, colonial civil servants and academics. Universities and centres of learning such as museums, medical schools, the Royal Geographical Society and the Royal Colonial Institute stored and disseminated the material gathered. Their work had a lasting impact on the way that the non-European world is viewed and formed the basis of subsequent scholarship, including Egyptology and anthropology. Thus, for example, museums and scholars in places

such as London continue to be regarded as world experts on the cultures and civilizations of distant lands, and when Western strategic interests lead government and military organizations to think about regions such as Waziristan or Somalia it is often to the pioneering work of early missionaries, anthropologists and district officers that they turn.

The process of gathering knowledge and developing understanding (or misunderstanding) of other lands and their peoples has been the subject of intense academic and moral debate. A clear link has been forged between knowledge and power, in this case the power to rule and dominate, and to make people in one part of the world feel superior to those in another, thus validating their ruling mission. Colonial knowledge was heavily engaged in the development of classificatory systems, and according to the work of scholars, writers and thinkers such as Edward Said, Michel Foucault and V.S. Naipaul a colonial view of the world came to rest at the very heart of Western culture and understanding.[1]

The process of knowledge-gathering saw indigenous cultures studied and appropriated by alien 'experts'. Explorers and missionaries were purveyors of Western ways, and accumulators and constructors of Western knowledge. That knowledge, together with the artefacts that supported it, was stored in the great institutional repositories back at home. Anthropologists such as Edward Evan Evans-Pritchard and Isaac Shapera codified 'native law and custom' and revealed how other people lived. A bank of knowledge about the world developed, as well as a rich collection of objects and documents in institutions such as the British Museum, the Imperial Institute, and the Pitt Rivers Museum and Rhodes House in Oxford. The activities of explorers, missionaries, scientists and scholars stimulated interest in distant parts of the world, firing imagination and entrepreneurship which created further threads in the dense web connecting 'over here' with 'over there'. In the nineteenth century evangelicals and utilitarians viewed the Empire as a vast laboratory in which social experiments leading towards general human 'upliftment' could be put into practice. For others, expanding horizons and technological developments meant that natural resources such as gold, oil and whale blubber could be located and harvested in more and more distant corners of the globe.

Through publications such as the Church Missionary Society's *Mission Papers* and public lectures supported by magic lantern displays, missionaries offered the public first-hand accounts of other countries and cultures, usually laced with a didactic message about why their customs and beliefs were inferior and in need of improvement. The knowledge the missionaries conveyed, however, was often extremely biased or simply inaccurate. Nevertheless, missionaries and religious organizations were adept at using new materials to bring images of the Empire and its people to the British public, and, as John MacKenzie points out, they had the necessary buildings in the form of church halls and chapels in which to show them. Missionaries such as Selwyn, Hannington and the great missionary-explorer Livingstone, who first ventured to Africa under the banner of the London Missionary Society, were celebrity figures, whilst General Gordon's strict Christian beliefs and unpleasant end meant that he qualified for national lionization both as a soldier and as a religious martyr.

The motives of the missionaries, their strident views of the world and what was 'right' and 'wrong' in it, and the arrogance with which they operated in other peoples' lands are traits not entirely absent in the West's dealings with the non-Western world today. Though usually genuine in their belief that they were doing good – bringing medicine and education as well as the Gospel – their influence is today considered questionable. They changed the way people lived and dressed, and played a role in demeaning other people's cultures and customs. On the more positive side, the anti-racist universalism that was a feature of the early-nineteenth-century missionary vision remains commendable to this day. It might be argued that some of the 'barbaric' practices that they sought to eradicate are still considered 'barbaric' and worthy of eradication, that the medicine they dispensed saved lives, and that their work to mitigate the worst impacts of European expansion (such as 'blackbirding' in the Pacific) deserves acknowledgement. Beyond this, the Christian message that they carried took root in diverse parts of the world, and missionary activity did almost as much to bring the Empire to Britain and the West as it did to purvey the West to the non-European world.

Legacies of the work of missionaries are still evident in many parts of the world, most obviously through the strength of Christian communities. In 2009 islanders in Vanuatu in the Pacific officially apologized to eighteen descendants of a missionary murdered and eaten in 1839. The Reverend John Williams met his end on the island of Irimenga in the group of islands that Captain Cook named the New Hebrides, after the rugged Scottish islands of which they reminded him. Unfortunately, the islands were being plundered by ruthless European traders seeking sandalwood, and Williams's arrival came only days after traders had killed some of the islanders. The murder of the missionary 'martyr' was widely reported in the British press. Pictures showed him being overcome by leaf-clad natives, the incident portrayed as yet another example of the savagery of the non-Europeans with whom Britain was increasingly in contact. The incident remained significant for the island for generations afterwards, and even 170 years later it was still believed that the island was cursed because of the murder. This was why the people were so keen to make redress to Williams's great-grandson and his relatives, symbolically offering them a seven-year-old child in exchange for the life that had been taken.

Explorers, alongside missionaries and soldiers, were probably the most visible representatives of overseas engagement in the nineteenth century. The 'discovery' of new lands, rivers, mountains, species and cultures contributed to Western cultural arrogance, but also to the development of more sympathetic perspectives on the problems facing non-Europeans (such as the slave trade which continued in the African interior long after the British had abandoned it). Exploration exoticized the wider world in the minds of the general public. From the eighteenth century the exploits of pioneering seafarers and landsmen were placed before the public in the form of dioramas, art displays and media coverage. The flora and fauna of Baffin Island were shown to the Glaswegian public, and Londoners were offered views of the Ganges and the South African veldt in art galleries and parks. The exploits of famous African explorers dominated the headlines in the nineteenth century, whilst in the twentieth century it was Arctic explorers such as Captain Scott who led the field (largely because these were the only large tracts of land that hadn't been widely explored and brought to the attention of the public).

The publications of missionaries and explorers, and their coverage in the press, meant that indigenous cultures were exposed to public view. People learned of the cultures and lifestyles of people living thousands of miles away. The work of artists supported this: early German engravings showed the people and the dwellings of New South Wales, whilst the hyperbole surrounding H.M. Stanley's travels in Africa led to a host of colourful publications and exhibitions. In places such as Tasmania, English artists discovered scenes that struck them in terms of their difference to and similarity with landscapes encountered back at home, and their canvases allowed people to visualize the new worlds in which British people were settling. When assessing the work of missionaries, explorers and other gatherers of knowledge about the non-European world, the amount of material that they generated shows how important they were in bringing the world to the British public. Even if it was not their intention, they were part of the force leading to European imperial expansion and the justification of imperial rule. As Susan Thorne succinctly puts it, 'ultimately, however righteous, missionary ideals constituted a double-edged sword that the defenders of empire were able to wield more successfully at home. The more passionately missionaries condemned colonial practice in light of sacred ideals, the more Britain's imperial mission would be associated with the intentions of the divine.'[2]

Abbildung einer Hutte in Neu Sudwales
(late eighteenth or early nineteenth century).

An early lithograph of a scene in Australia. The
German inscription reads 'Illustration of a Hut in
New South Wales'.

JJ Empire & Colonies Box 1

Abbildung einer Hutte in Neu Sudwales.

A familiar imperial figure, the missionary-clergyman (1878).

The Right Reverend George Augustus Selwyn was the nineteenth Bishop of Lichfield and first Bishop of New Zealand, an instructive example of the connection between English towns and counties and distant colonial territories. These links are also illustrated by the fact that this picture was presented with *The Derbyshire Times* upon the bishop's death in May 1878. In the fifteen years following his death, both Selwyn College, Cambridge and Selwyn College, Otago were named after him. Selwyn had rowed in the first ever Oxford–Cambridge Boat Race in 1829, and his fame demonstrates the prominence of missionaries and overseas sees in the British Empire. He was instrumental in the spread of Christianity and also in the creation of the Dominion of New Zealand. The author Charles Kingsley dedicated *Westward Ho!* (1855) to both Selwyn and James Brooke, the first white rajah of Sarawak, because he considered them to be exemplary specimens of Englishmen abroad. Sir James Brooke (1803–1868) was born in India and entered into the military service of the East India Company. In 1841 he took an armed schooner to Sarawak in Borneo, intending to found a settlement. There he helped the Sultan of Brunei's uncle suppress a rebellion, and was rewarded with the governorship of Sarawak and the title 'rajah'. Until 1946, when Sarawak became a British colony, Brooke and his descendants continued to rule. In 1847 the British government made him governor of the recently annexed Labuan, and he was also appointed British Consul General to Borneo and knighted in 1848.

JJ Empire & Colonies Box 1

Missionary Papers

FOR THE USE OF THE
WEEKLY AND MONTHLY CONTRIBUTORS
TO THE
CHURCH MISSIONARY SOCIETY.

NEW-ZEALAND FIGURES.

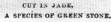

CUT IN JADE,
A SPECIES OF GREEN STONE.

CARVED IN WOOD.

CHRISTIAN FRIENDS—
  We shall, in this Number, give you a
FURTHER ACCOUNT OF THE NEW ZEALANDERS.

In our last Number, you might learn the ingenuity and skill of the New Zealanders, from the pictures which it contained, of the Head of Shunghee, and the Signature of Ahoodee O Gunna.

Is it not strange, that men of such manly aspect, and such native ability, should have associations in their minds, of which the above uncouth figures are the expression? Here you may learn, that, however skilful men may be, when they glorify not God, they *become vain in their imaginations, and their foolish heart is darkened*; and they *change the glory of the uncorruptible God into an image made like to corruptible man.*

There are different accounts of these Figures. The Figure on the left hand is taken from one cut in jade, a species of green stone. Mr. Savage, in his account of New Zealand, has given a plate of one. They are frequently to be met with in this country. They are very commonly worn about the necks of the Chiefs and their wives, particularly in time of danger.

Mr. Savage says, that this Figure is intended for a likeness of a Protecting Deity, whom they believe to dwell in the Moon; which planet is, in consequence, the favourite object of their adoration. They have a notion that the Moon is the abode of a man, who, at some distant period, paid a visit to New Zealand, and who is still very anxious for its welfare and that of its inhabitants. It is possible that the New Zealanders may fancy that they can discover on the face of the Moon some traces of this uncouth figure.

No. IV. *Christmas*, 1816.

Missionary Papers (1816).

An interesting example of the role played by missionaries in gathering knowledge from the colonial world and purveying it to people in Britain. The *Missionary Papers* of the Church Missionary Society were sent to those who supported its work overseas. This edition from Christmas 1816 shows Maori artefacts crafted from jade and wood, and offers an account of New Zealand's indigenous people. The text strikes a typical moralizing tone; the figures are adjudged to be 'uncouth' because – although the Maoris possessed 'ingenuity and skill' – 'they glorify not God'. Though skewed by an uncompromising and 'civilizing' Christianity, such accounts offered an explanation of alien cultures to people back in Britain.

JJ Empire & Colonies Box 1

A drawing from the *Missionary Papers* of the Church Missionary Society showing a Maori chief, midsummer 1826.

The chief, Tooi, who toured Britain in 1818, had been brought to Britain aboard HMS *Kangaroo*, an initiative of the Church Missionary Society's representatives, Samuel Marsden and Thomas Kendall. Marsden had first arrived in the Bay of Islands aboard the schooner *Active* in 1814, and claimed to have been the first man to conduct a Christian service in the country. The chief of the Nagpuhi tribe at the time, Ruatara, invited the Society to build a mission station in his territory. But this didn't necessarily denote success for the missionaries: it appears that the chief was more interested in the access to Western technology, including firearms, that this contact might facilitate. Along with his people, Chief Ruatara remained impervious to the message of the Gospel for many years to come.

JJ Empire & Colonies Box 1

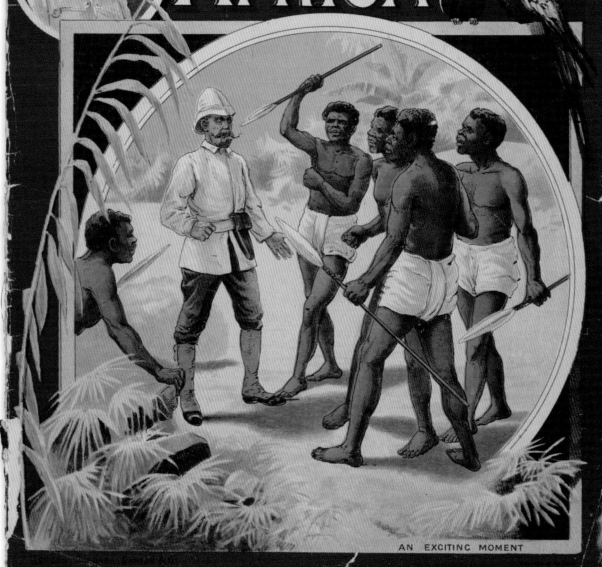

ARTON'S

HEROES IN
AFRICA

AN EXCITING MOMENT

**'An exciting moment':
The cover of Darton's *Heroes in Africa*, c.1890.** (*left*)

This colourful brochure presented a standard contemporary view of the 'opening up' of Africa and the beneficent role of British missionaries and explorers in a region of the world then considered to be marred by savagery and slavery. It opens with the words: 'Twenty years ago the map of Africa was very different from what it is now. All the centre was marked "unexplored". Now it is almost covered with the names of tribes, towns, mountains, and rivers. It is no longer the "Dark Continent". It has been opened up by Livingstone, Stanley, Baker, and many others.'

JJ Empire & Colonies Box 5

***Stanley in Africa*
(*c.*1890s).** (*right*)

Number 14 in Dean's Gold Medal Series, a colourful magazine showcasing and glorifying the exploits of the controversial journalist and explorer Henry Morton Stanley (1841–1904).

JJ Empire & Colonies Box 5

DEAN'S GOLD MEDAL SERIES Nº 14.

STANLEY in AFRICA

LONDON,
Dean & Son, 160ᴬ Fleet St.

Darton's *Heroes in Africa* (c. 1890).

These colour pictures illustrate the manner in which ideas about Africa were formed in the public mind, inaccurate though they were – note the 'land of dwarfs' description. The stories present common, albeit false, assumptions about Africa and the role of Europeans in it, assumptions that were used to justify and underpin the presence of Europeans and the expansion of their colonial holdings. A common assumption was that only European action could end the evils of the slave trade, humanitarianism justifying empire. Of course, not all Africans welcomed the presence of Europeans, though this was depicted as little more than a manifestation of African backwardness; see the drawing 'attacked by natives' (*left*).

JJ Empire & Colonies Box 5

A SLAVE CARAVAN.

to keep up a running fight for several days when he was descending the River Congo. You cannot go far into Africa without meeting a slave caravan; it is a very sad sight. As you go through the forest you hear the sound of drums, and presently you see the caravan coming. First the slave dealer, riding on a donkey, with his wives and household slaves following him, and then the slaves and their drivers, men, women, and children, torn from

their happy homes, and fastened together with ropes and logs of wood, carrying burdens of ivory, or other articles of trade, on their

REDEEMING TWO SLAVE BOYS.

shoulders, and all weary, footsore, half-starved, and bleeding from the blows they have received. Scarcely more than one in five lives to reach the slave market. The slave trade is going on now almost as bad as ever. Anyone who will go out to try to stop it would be doing a hero's work.

THE LAND OF DWARFS.

INTERESTING NOVELTY,

Never before Exhibited in Aberdeen.

Frozen Regions, Bannockburn,

&c. *March 1833*

Ducrow's Amphitheatre, Crown Street.

Boxes, 1s.—Gallery, 6d.

Day Exhibitions, at One and Two o'Clock.—Evening do. at Seven and half-past Eight o'Clock.

Mr. MARSHALL, grateful for the liberal patronage received, begs to intimate, that as the Amphitheatre is to be pulled down, and from its great width and capaciousness being admirably adapted for exhibiting to advantage his Panorama of the FROZEN REGIONS, he has therefore availed himself of this opportunity, which may never occur again, and has Opened, for a few days, his highly-interesting Panorama of

Eight Views of Captains Parry, Ross, Franklin, and Buchan's Voyages of Discovery

IN THE

POLAR REGIONS.

Displaying the North Coast of Spitzbergen, Baffin's Bay, Melville Island, Arctic Highlands, &c.

Painted from Drawings made on the spot, by Lieut. Beechy, Messrs. Fisher, Ross, &c. who accompanied the Expedition, and is completely illustrative of the Sublime and Novel Scenery, the Natives, Birds, Beasts, &c. of that remote Country.

To which is added, the National HISTORICAL PANORAMA of

Four Views of the ever-memorable Battle of

Bannockburn,

Fought on Sunday, 24th June, 1314, by King Robert the Bruce.
Painted principally from the suggestions and under the direction of the late Sir Walter Scott, Bart.
The Localities sketched from Nature, on the spot.

The whole painted on 19,000 Square Feet of Canvas—the Figures and Horses being the size of life, the Ships on the largest scale, and being accompanied by appropriate Music and Description—forms an Exhibition of great interest, and of the most rational amusement; and is the last Panorama that will be exhibited here this Season.

ORDER OF THE SUBJECTS, AND MUSICAL ACCOMPANIMENTS.
NORTH COAST OF SPITZBERGEN.

1st.—His Majesty's Ship the Dorothea, Captain Buchan, in the vicinity of Cloven Cliff, nipped between two Floes of Ice, while attempting to force her way to the edge of the tremendous Icy Barrier; Capts. Buchan and Franklin, and Mr. Fisher, the Astronomer, are making observations.—Music, " *Rule Britannia.*"

2d.—His Majesty's Ship the Trent, Capt. Franklin, pressed between two Fields of Ice, heeling over. The Crew are endeavouring to extricate her by carrying out ropes, anchors, &c. In this View the Ice Blink is represented, besides groupes of Seals, Walrusses, Eider Ducks, Terns, &c.—Music, " *Hearts of Oak.*"

3d & 4th.—Red Hill with the surrounding magnificent Scenery peculiar to this Frozen Climate, part of the Crew on the Floating Ice, killing Walrusses, or Sea Horses.—Music, " *All's Well.*

5th.—Red Bay, three Icebergs, Capt. Franklin and part of the Crew in a Boat shooting Polar Bears.—Music, " *Heaving of the Lead.*"

6th.—The Islands named the Norways, Cloven Cliff, and Vogel Sang, with the adjacent country.—Music, " *See from Ocean Rising.*"

BAFFIN'S BAY, &c.

7th.—His Majesty's Ship the Isabella, Capt. Ross, and the Alexander, Capt. Parry, at the newly-discovered land in Baffin's Bay, named the Arctic Highlands, Capts. Ross and Parry, Saccheuse, the Esquimaux, and some of the Crew upon the Ice giving presents, and in conference with the Natives, numbers of whom are also seen in their sledges, drawn by dogs, &c.—Music, " *Indian Dance.*"

8th.—Crimson Cliffs, &c. Capts. Parry and Ross, Saccheuse, and part of the Crews, playing at football with the Natives on the Ice.—" Music, " *Heigh Yaw Waltz.*"

BATTLE OF BANNOCKBURN.

9th.—King Robert the Bruce and Suite on the Brocks Brae. The ancient City and Castle of Stirling in the distance,—part of the Scottish Reserve, and the advance of Sir Robert Keith's select body of Cavalry against the English Archers.—Music, " *Scots wha hae wi' Wallace bled.*"

10th.—The Overthrow of the English Archers, and 10,000 English Cavalry in the pits,—the left wing of the Scottish Army, under Randolph, Earl of Moray, coming up against them.—Music, " *March to the Battle Field.*"

11th.—The Death of the Earl of Gloucester,—Edward II. the English King and suite preparing to quit the Field.—Music, " *The Scots came over the Border.*"

12th.—The Gillies Hill,—the advance of the Scottish Camp, male and female, with the complete Overthrow of the English Army.—**FINALE, " God Save the King."**

Public notice dating from March 1833, advertising exhibitions in Aberdeen.
(*left*)

This notice illustrates the manner in which ordinary people encountered images and information regarding distant parts of the world and the exploits of British explorers, traders and soldiers. Alongside an exhibition on the Battle of Bannockburn, the main feature was a show about the polar regions, drawn from the voyages of captains Parry, Ross, Franklin and Buchanan. The images, 'painted on the spot' and therefore authentic, showed 'novel scenery, the natives, birds, beasts, of that remote country'. The lands covered by the voyages included Spitzbergen and 'the newly discovered land in Baffin's Bay'. The pictures were accompanied by stirring music; thus when members of the crew of HMS *Isabella* are depicted at the naming of the 'Arctic Highlands', in the company of 'Natives' ('numbers of whom are also seen in their sledges, drawn by dogs'), the song *Indian Dance* was played.

JJ Exploration Box

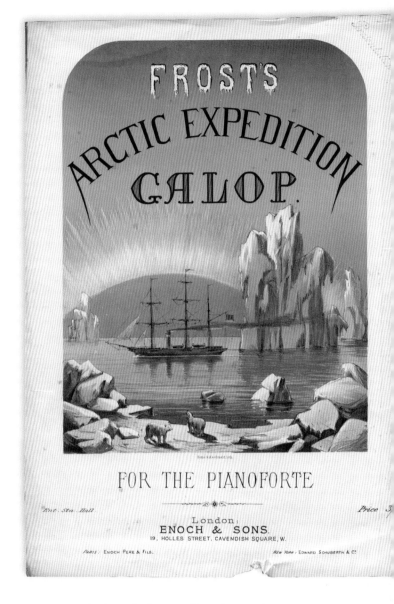

Sheet music for William L. Frost's 'Arctic Expedition Galop for the Pianoforte' (1876).

JJ Exploration Box

89

***Illustrated London News*, 'India Supplement', 28 November 1857.**

The Indian Mutiny had broken out in May 1857, and continued to shock the British public. Its suppression took many months and required the gathering of imperial forces from Britain, the Cape, Mauritius, Persia and elsewhere. Note the fine detail of the banner and the elaboration of the article's first letter. This article on the 'History of the British Empire in India' reflects the fact that the British government and people were now to take over the management of India's affairs, as the Mutiny had already led to the abolition of the East India Company, which since the seventeenth century had been the primary mechanism of British governance on the subcontinent. The British government and people were now responsible for 'over one hundred and fifty millions of the poorest and most benighted people under the face of the sun'. 'England must accept the charge – first, to reconquer what is well-nigh lost, and reconstruct the fabric of society, tottering amid misrule and treason... In short, we must, for the first time, occupy and colonise these our vast possessions, firmly, wisely, completely; and this we must do at whatever cost of blood and treasure.'

JJ Empire & Colonies Folder

No. 890.]   NOVEMBER 28, 1857.   [VOL. XXXI.

HISTORY OF THE BRITISH EMPIRE IN INDIA.

INTRODUCTION.

BRITISH rule in India is but an infant institution amongst the great family of nations. Although it is somewhat more than two centuries and a half since the first Company of Merchants was formed in London for the purpose of "trading with all countries between the Cape of Good Hope and the Straits of Magellan," we cannot claim anything in the nature of an empire in Hindostan [from an earlier date than a hundred years back. Small and precarious as were the first efforts of the company, its subsequent growth has in great measure been the result of accident and fortuitous circumstances, alike uncalculated upon and uncontrolled by those whose destiny it was to guard its interests; for, as will be seen by the sequel, it is a fact that, owing to their distance from the scene of operations, and the wayward nature of the agents appointed by them, the East India Company, who were the parties most immediately interested in these concerns, often knew very little of what was doing in their name and on their behalf until it

was over, and that too frequently what was done was in direct opposition to their positive behests. As to the Government of the country, which had an ultimate interest and responsibility in the affairs of this new empire mysteriously growing up in the Eastern Hemisphere, it was, until very recently, so engrossed with cares and dangers nearer home that it paid very little attention to the subject; saving to put in a claim now and then for a modest share of any plunder realised, little dreaming at what cost those perquisitions would one day have to be paid for. The East India Company's Regulation Act, passed in the year 1769, was the first faint recognition by the Imperial Government of its prerogatives and duties in this matter. The Act of 1784 went further, but still left the matter, in all its practical bearings, in a most unsatisfactory state. The clumsy double jurisdiction established by it was but an expedient to obtain power, patronage, and control, whilst ingeniously avoiding responsibility.

As for the people of England during all this time, their knowledge of India has been most loose and general, limited, in most cases, to vague notions of a great Mogul, turbaned Nabobs, black soldiers, Cashmere shawls, Trichinopoly chains, elephants' teeth, curry-powder, cadetships, and liver complaint. Through all this misshapen chaos of various strange forms loomed a not very definite impression, encouraged by the East India Directors, and tacitly indulged in by Ministers and the public at large, that India was a mine of inexhaustible wealth, entitling it to be esteemed one of the brightest jewels in the Imperial diadem. From time to time, it is true, rumours of temporary disaster, and indications of a pressing requirement of pecuniary assistance on the part of the East India Company, served to qualify the sweets and glories of this gratifying prospect, but only sufficiently so to realise the universally-acknowledged truth that no

earthly blessing is perfect and unalloyed, and thus to give the zest of stern reality to the possession.

We are now called upon, and called in terrible accents, to awake from this delusive dream. The nation's honour and the nation's interests are henceforth involved in the affairs of the Company of Merchants (until recently) trading to India, and holding conclave, and dispensing patronage, in Leadenhall-street. Their estate in India has fallen away from them—it devolves upon us whether we like it or not; their empire over one million and a quarter of square miles of the richest and most neglected territory, and over one hundred and fifty millions of the poorest and most benighted people under the face of the sun, has crumbled away beneath them, and we, the people of England, must accept the charge—first, to reconquer what is well-nigh lost, and reconstruct the fabric of society, tottering amid misrule and treason; and then to reimprove the natural gifts of soil, too long neglected, and create friendly and profitable intercourse between our new subjects and the various distant nations of the earth. In short, we must, for the first time, occupy and colonise these our vast possessions, firmly, wisely, completely; and this we must do at whatever cost of blood and treasure.

With a task like this before us, in which every man, in person or purse, must bear his share, it behoves us all to consider maturely what it is we have to deal with—what the antecedents, what the prospects, of the case. There is no branch of the external relations of the country about which more has been written and said than India. Unfortunately, however, the major part of the publications and discussions upon this subject have been so diffuse and so loaded with matters of official and technical detail as to be ineligible for purposes of general study. Another circumstance which has served to prevent a wider consideration and juster appreciation of the true bearings of this subject, amongst even

Monsoon Fishing in Bombay Harbour, 1838

'**Monsoon fishing in Bombay harbour, 1838', a special publication commemorating** *The Times of India*'**s centenary.**

The supplement features an essay by S.T. Sheppard entitled 'India 100 Years Ago', which offers a standard account of how the coming of British rule had led to a revolution in communications and development which had propelled India into the modern world. The message was uncomplicated: India needs Britain, and British rule is good.

JJ Empire & Colonies Box 2

State inauguration of the Imperial Institute, 10 May 1893.

Taken from the souvenir programme published for the inauguration of the Imperial Institute in 1893, this illustration shows the elaborate ceremonial key with which the Queen–Empress opened the building. Built between 1887 and 1893, the Imperial Institute was located on Exhibition Road in South Kensington. The Queen had laid the foundation stone in 1887 whilst Arthur Sullivan (of Gilbert and Sullivan fame) conducted his *Imperial Ode*. The idea for such an Institute had been conceived during the Colonial and Indian Exhibition of 1886, and it was dedicated to scientific and commercial research. The decorative key is typical of the inventiveness of the age, in which new things were steeped in 'tradition' and symbolism, and is reminiscent of the design that went into creating new imperial honours in the late nineteenth and early twentieth centuries. In the case of this ornate key, one side (*left*) is the Indian face, showing the Insignia of the Order of the Star of India, the other (*right*) the Colonial face, showing the Insignia of the Order of St Michael and St George (the main order in the honours system for those serving in the colonies). The key shows the Imperial Crown, Maltese crosses, the fleurs-de-lys of the Royal Coronet, and the rose, thistle and shamrock of the home nations (no leeks, apparently, were available). The gold, silver and diamonds were contributed by colonial governments and India – gold from South Africa and British Colombia, silver, gold, and green gold from the Australian colonies, rubies from Burma, pearls from Ceylon, and diamonds from South Africa. 'The Queen will insert and turn the key in a lock fixed upon a pedestal upon which rests the silver model of the Imperial Institute presented by the Corporation of the City of London to the Prince and Princess of Wales on the occasion of their Silver Wedding. This operation will cause a bolt to fall and complete an electrical circuit; a signal will be thereby given to the central or "Queen's Tower", whereupon the "Alexandra" peal of bells will for the first time be rung.' Reassuringly, to the security-conscious, the key was constructed by none other than Sir George Chubb. All that remains of the Imperial Institute today is the 85 metre Queen's Tower, which forms part of Imperial College London, to which the other original buildings gave way in the 1950s and 1960s.

JJ Ceremonial Box 4

KEY TO BE USED BY

Ḷer ᙏajesty Ḡhe Queen

AT THE INAUGURATION OF THE IMPERIAL INSTITUTE,
10TH MAY, 1893.

Case for Key.

*Indian face, showing
the Insignia of the
Order of the Star
of India.*

*Colonial face, showing
the Insignia of the
Order of St. Michael
and St. George.*

This Key which is to be presented to Queen Victoria on the occasion of the Opening Ceremony will be employed by Her Majesty during the Ceremonial to symbolise the inauguration of the Imperial Institute.

The Queen will insert and turn the key in a lock fixed upon a pedestal upon which rests the silver model of the Imperial Institute presented by the Corporation of the City of London to the Prince and Princess of Wales on the occasion of their Silver Wedding. This operation will cause a bolt to fall and complete an electric circuit; a signal will be thereby given to the central or "Queen's" Tower, whereupon the "Alexandra" peal of bells will for the first time be rung.

The gold, silver and diamonds, of which the key is composed, have been contributed by several Colonial Governments and by India, so that different portions of the British Empire are represented by its various component parts. The head of the key is formed of gold from South Africa, and of silver from the Broken Hill Mine, Australia; the stem is composed of gold from British Columbia; while the bitt and wards consist of the precious metal from Queensland Mines. The stem of the key is encircled by a riband in red gold and a wreath of laurel leaves in green gold, both obtained from Victoria, while gold from that Colony composes the ornaments upon the lid of the case which contains the key. The diamonds in the key and ornaments are from South Africa; the rubies from Burmah; and the pearls from Ceylon.

The circular head of the key is surmounted by the Imperial Crown; the outer border is composed of Maltese Crosses with the fleurs-de-lis of the Royal Coronet. This border joins the stem of the key by descending curves, decorated with shields and the national symbols, Rose, Thistle and Shamrock, in enamel. The obverse shield bears the Arms of the United Kingdom; the reverse those of England alone. The two sides of the head are reduced, but accurate, representations of the Grand Cross of the Order of the Star of India, and the Grand Cross of the Order of St. Michael and St. George. The Star of India has a fine diamond star of five points in the centre.

The stem of the key is richly diversified with mouldings, the inscription on the riband being:— "Imperial Institute; commenced 1887, inaugurated 1893." The decorated wards of the key form the letters I.I., the initial letters of the Imperial Institute. On the rim of the key-head is the inscription:—"Presented to Victoria, Queen-Empress, on the occasion of the opening of the Imperial Institute, 10 May, 1893."

The Case of the key is in Royal Blue Velvet, with a paler blue lining, and has on the lid an ornament composed of the Royal Crown set with diamonds, rubies and pearls, and beneath it the Orb set with fine stones of pure colour, the Royal Sceptre and the Sceptre of Peace being placed behind it, with a laurel wreath encircling all. Inside the case, a gold shield surmounted by the Crown bears an inscription of sources from whence the gems and precious metals of which the key is made have been obtained.

The key has been produced under the direction of **Sir George Chubb**, with whom originated the suggestion that it should be constructed of Colonial and Indian metals and jewels.

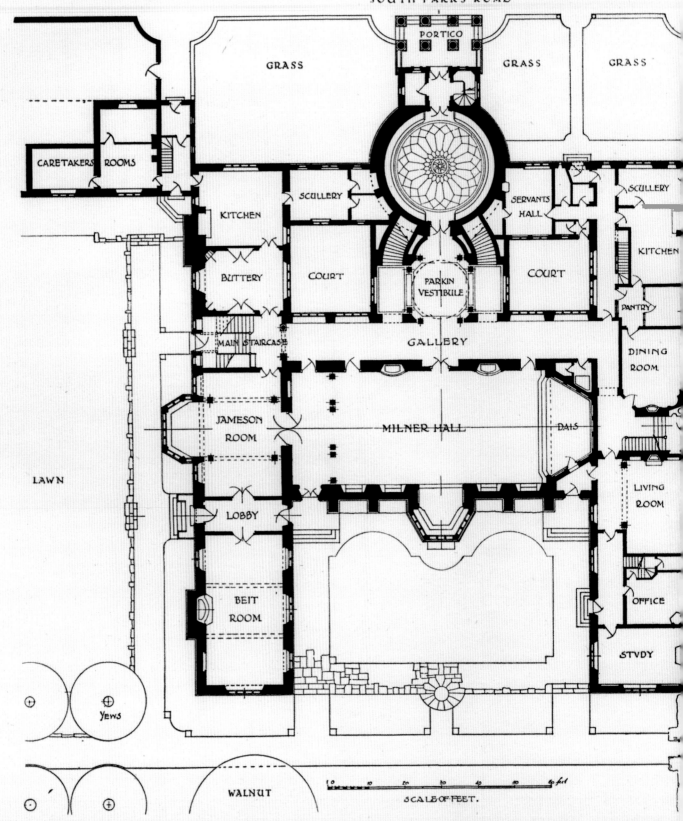

SOUTH PARKS ROAD

GRASS

PORTICO

GRASS

GRASS

CARETAKERS ROOMS

KITCHEN

SCULLERY

SERVANTS HALL

SCULLERY

KITCHEN

BUTTERY

COURT

PARKIN VESTIBULE

COURT

PANTRY

DINING ROOM

MAIN STAIRCASE

GALLERY

JAMESON ROOM

MILNER HALL

DAIS

LAWN

LIVING ROOM

LOBBY

BEIT ROOM

OFFICE

STVDY

YEWS

WALNUT

SCALE OF FEET.

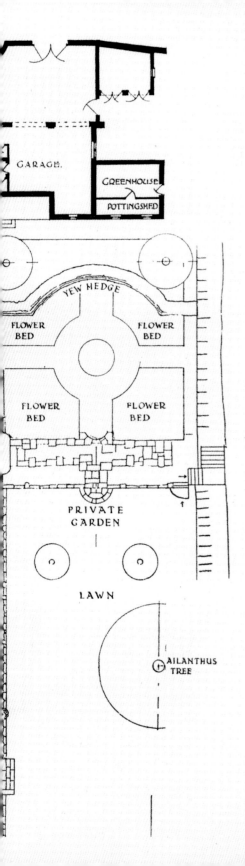

GARAGE.

GREENHOUSE

POTTINGSHED

YEW HEDGE

FLOWER BED   FLOWER BED

FLOWER BED   FLOWER BED

PRIVATE GARDEN

LAWN

AILANTHUS TREE

A ground plan of Rhodes House in Oxford (1932).

This building represents the accumulation of knowledge about the wider world within Britain, as well as Cecil Rhodes's desire to form an anglicized global elite through the Rhodes Trust and its scholarships. The building was also a memorial for Rhodes and his friends, containing paintings and busts of men such as Sir Alfred Milner, George Parkin, Leander Starr Jameson and Alfred Beit. The brochure *Cecil Rhodes and Rhodes House* was published by Oxford University Press in 1932 (and printed by the University Printer, John Johnson, the originator of the John Johnson Collection). 'This house', it proclaimed, 'stands for ever a reminder of the name and example of Cecil John Rhodes to the Oxford he loved.' It still does, amidst the lawns fringed with alianthus, yew and walnut. It remains the headquarters of the Rhodes Trust, and the University's main library and archive of African and Commonwealth material.

JJ Empire & Colonies Box 4

IMPERIAL TRADE, COMMERCE AND MARKETING

The evolution of vigorous settler societies contributed to the growth of a new international economy based on commodity trade, the exchange of manufactured goods for raw materials, and the spread of new financial institutions. Many leading British companies have their roots in the expansion of the British Empire and the products of the wider world, including BP (formerly Anglo-Persian Oil), Cadbury, HSBC (the Hong Kong and Shanghai Banking Corporation), Tate & Lyle and Unilever. The transport by sea of raw materials and finished goods was the lifeblood of the British Empire, as the 'workshop of the world' became its leading importer and exporter, shipper and banker. The images in this chapter reflect the growth of an imperial economy, including the initiatives of those who sought to transform the Empire into a formal economic zone or trading bloc surrounded by protectionist walls.

Trade, often conducted on an unequal footing and sometimes tantamount to plunder, was a defining feature of the British Empire and its growth. Empire and the expansion of industrial economies were major globalizing forces, as raw materials from the non-Western world were transported to industrial heartlands and manufactured goods moved in the other direction. Thus, in one of the most notorious cases of economic exploitation, the textile industry of India was degraded as the finished products of Lancashire's mills flooded the Asian market. Luxury goods produced in the Empire and the semi-colonized world became necessities at home. Tobacco imports from the colonies grew from 30 million lb in 1700 to about 76 million lb in 1800.[1] Sugar from the colonies was consumed at the rate of 4 lb per head of the British population each year in the 1690s, a figure that had risen to 24 lb by the 1790s. In 1913, 80 per cent of Britain's wheat and 45 per cent of its meat and dairy produce came from overseas.

Egyptian cotton, West Indian and Mauritian sugar, South American beef, North American grain and Far Eastern silk and tea were key overseas products for the British economy. Moving in the other direction, the British exported capital to investment-hungry developing countries, as well as manufactured goods, coal, beer and consumer products. Captain William Bligh was responsible for taking breadfruit from the Pacific to the West Indies, where it became an established crop, whilst tea was transplanted from China to Ceylon and India so that the British could have their 'own' supply and stop having to pay for it in bullion. As a result of this transplantation, the quantity of tea imported from China went down, whilst that imported from Assam and Ceylon shot up: by 1900 Assam and Ceylon accounted for 90 per cent of British tea imports and China 10 per cent, inverting the percentages that had pertained a century before.[2] According to some economic historians the Empire acted as a cushion for British industry as it became less competitive from the late nineteenth century, delaying necessary modernization and hastening industrial decline. Whilst this debate is not important here, the imperial dimension of Britain's modern economic history is noteworthy.

In the early days of British overseas expansion the East India Company was a giant force in world trade and a significant factor in the British domestic economy. The Company made vast sums of money importing silks, spices and other luxury goods, whilst British firms exported goods to Asia. The economic activities of the Company also made a great deal of money for the British Treasury. The Company had its own navy and merchant marine, all controlled from East India House in the City of London. It had warehouses in Wandsworth and 'factories' overseas, both on the Indian subcontinent and at waystations on the route to the East such as the Cape and St Helena. The Company was granted control over the administration of huge areas of India and permitted a military capability that most nation-states would have envied. Gradually it came under the control of the British government, as the British became more aware of the implications of possessing such a large and growing Oriental domain and as the Company's financial affairs and administrative methods came to require regulation. In the year after the Indian Mutiny of 1857, the British Crown took over responsibility for the Indian empire from the East India Company, and in 1877 Prime Minister Benjamin Disraeli created Victoria 'Empress of India'.

The manner in which Indian affairs obtruded in British moral and political debate is illustrated by the use of the word 'nabob'. The word had been used in English since the early seventeenth century, a corruption of the Hindi *nawab*, meaning governor or person of wealth and status. Seldom heard today, it was once much more common. It was used to describe the East India Company employees who had spent time out East and profited by 'shaking the pagoda tree'. The moral and political problems began when they brought their wealth home and set themselves up in style. Questions were asked: was it right that they should have profited from what had often been ill-gotten gains? Was it right that British people working for a chartered company should be increasingly involved in ruling people of different culture? If so, rather than conducting business among them, surely it was more important to take the word of the Lord to them and improve their social and economic practices? Furthermore, was it right that these Eastern-enriched merchants, these nabobs, should be allowed to convert their wealth into landed estates at home, which translated into political power and higher social status?

Oceanic trade routes were a defining feature of the Empire and the manner in which it was explained to the public. The Royal Navy was commonly presented as protecting the globe's trade routes, for the good of Britain and the world. Thus it was easy to present Britain's possession of the world's greatest navy as a necessity of benefit to Britain and the whole world, whilst the navies of other powers, especially when they threatened to challenge British supremacy, were castigated as 'luxuries' likely to lead to conflict as opposed to the preservation of peace. Trade routes and imperial networks were often represented on maps of the world and were a primary way in which the public encountered illustrations of the Empire. An intriguing Canadian map showed Canada (as opposed to Britain) at the centre of the world, and boldly proclaimed that the dominion 'stood astride the world's trade routes'. Shipping lines advertised their services as the British merchant marine carried trade goods and raw materials all over the world. In 1803 there were over 18,000 ships of various sizes registered in Britain. Global shipping supported a huge number of businesses. Gordon & Gotch, for example, published *The Australian Handbook Shippers' and Importers' Directory*, and marketed themselves as experts in the facilitation of advertisement in the colonies.

Consumer culture was already well developed when the British Empire reached its zenith in the nineteenth century. Many consumer

5
ORANGE GROWING
SOUTH AFRICA

Reproduction from an Empire Marketing Board poster

Thirty years ago oranges were only to be had here in winter and early spring. Now South Africa supplies us with oranges all through the summer.

products came from the territories of the Empire or used imperial and wider-world imagery to boost sales. Dried fruit, rubber, tea, coffee, chocolate, sugar, peaches, pineapples, cotton and tobacco were quintessentially imperial products, whether or not the British public knew or particularly cared. Certain products were always closely identified with empire and the wider world, because of their nature or the manner in which they were marketed. Curry powder, chutney and arrowroot were features of the British larder from the eighteenth century. Bovril was marketed with an imperial and patriotic edge, and Coleman's used images from the Raj to sell its mustard. In the mid-twentieth century, Ford cars attempted to harness the cachet of the British Empire in advertisements.

In the interwar period the government-sponsored Empire Marketing Board attempted to raise the profile of empire products through poster campaigns, shopping weeks and even card games, intended to stimulate intra-imperial trade during the Depression. Trade fairs and imperial exhibitions provided promotional opportunities for colonial governments to sell their wares to the British public. There were also trade fairs in the colonies themselves, such as the 1927 Calabar Trade Fair in Nigeria. Developing business networks took supermarkets to the colonies, and special advertisements were designed to sell British and colonial products to Africans and Asians.

In the twentieth century, the empire remained a source of rubber goods, dairy products, fruit and medicines. Famous brands of soap, cocoa and drinks associated themselves with patriotism and empire. The accession of Elizabeth II led to a renewed focus on the 'Elizabethan inheritance' of a global trading community. The Empire was portrayed as a place of growing development and an attractive option for investors, as British governments in the 1950s looked to imperial markets and the dollar-earning potential of the Empire to help Britain recover from the debilitating effects of the Second World War. Trade and economic links to the British Commonwealth remained a feature of intra-Commonwealth relations until late in the twentieth century. Britain's entry into the European Economic Community in 1973 caused consternation in the former dominions and was seen as a breaking point, as the British economy acknowledged its reorientation towards Europe. Significant ties, however, remain, as well as preferential agreements for former colonial territories such as those provided under the European Union's Lomé Conventions.

A Particular of Goods to be expofed to Sale by the East-India Company, *in* September, 1676. *Viz.*

Pieces.

Callicoes {
23890 Long Clothes White
9465 Ditto Brown
3200 Ditto Blew
46954 Salampores White
3835 Ditto Brown
16539 Percallaes
15680 Morees
9326 Ginghams
5515 Ditto Coloured
1550 Izzarees
1320 Diapers
2473 Bettelees White
107 Ditto Brown
8280 Ditto Oringal
640 Neck-clothes
5900 Allejaes
133 Sheets
8382 Dungarees
28333 Sannoes
1236 Humhums
2902 Coffaes
1323 Mulmulls
5700 Taffaties
2430 Ditto Raw
6593 Nillaes
920 Quilts large
400 Ditto fmall
1440 Chints large Eranch
6560 Ditto Broad
7400 Ditto Narrow
3200 Ditto Serunge
7680 Ditto Caddy
5809 Tapfeiles Broad
5040 Ditto Narrow
4435 Niccances
9600 Guinea Stuffs
9300 Brawles
22992 Pautkaes White
9070 Ditto Frown
3400 Ditto Blew
982 Dungarees White
81 Ditto Brown
570 Derebands Small
Bi amrauts
}

Callicoes {
35305 Bafts Broad White
6520 Ditto Blew
1755 Ditto Brown
37900 Ditto Narrow White
1605 Ditto Erown
43 Parcallaes
561 Geelings
43 Mufters
}

Silk {
Raw Silk Bengale ———— Bales 108
Raw Silk China ———— 24
Stitching Silk Dyed ———— 2
Floretta Yarn ———— 40
1601 Cordivant skins
}

Musk in Cod ———— Pots 3
Pepper Black ———— Ba. 7886
Ditto White ———— 344
Ditto Damaged and Duft ———— 19
Cotton Yarn ———— 352
Carmenia Wooll ———— 318
Coffee ———— 106

Druggs {
Cardemoms ———— 209
Olibanum ———— 143
Seedlack ———— 4
Sticklack ———— 161
Turmerick ———— 363
Rice ———— 320
Cowrees ———— 500
Saltpetre ———— 5000
Ditto Fine ———— 408
China Roots ———— 108
Canifters 78
Indico Lahore ———— Barrels 275
Ditto Cirques flat ———— 106
Ditto round ———— 3
Indico Duft ———— 37
Benjamin ———— Chefts 42
Lapis Tutiæ ———— 13
Salarmoniack ———— 51
Green Ginger ———— Jars 579
Tincal ———— Drppers 184
Sapan Wood ———— Sticks 1
Sandal Wood ———— C
Red Earth ————
130 Buffloe Hides
631 Indico Skins
6 1 Shirts
}

Advertisement listing East India trade goods shipped from India for sale in London (September 1676).

This advertisement gives an impression of the type of goods involved in the burgeoning trade between Asia and Europe. Cloth is much in evidence, as are spices.

JJ East India Company Box 1

**'The East India House,
Drawn & Engrav'd by S. Rawle' (1803).**

This image appeared in the *European Magazine*
in April 1803. East India House on Leadenhall
Street was completed in 1729 to the designs of
the merchant and architect Theodore Jacobsen
(d. 1772). From here, the Directors of the East India
Company ruled over vast tracts of the subcontinent
until the Company was abolished after the Indian
Mutiny and governance transferred to the British
Crown. Above the Doric pilasters was a frieze of
treglyphs, symbolizing the prudence and wisdom
of the Company in pursuit of its shareholders'
interests. The Directors' Court Room featured a
bas-relief panel of 'Britannia Receiving the Riches
of the East' by Michael Rysbrack (1693-1770),
though it is fair to say that Company rule was to
be remembered more for 'taking' than 'receiving'.
The room also contained six canvases depicting the
Company's major factories in Bombay, Cape Town,
Fort William, Madras, St Helena and Tellicherry.
The building was sold in 1868 and demolished in the
following year. The Lloyd's Building now occupies
the site.

JJ East India Company Box 1

The Indian Store Department, Belvedere Road, Lambeth (1868).

Britain's relationship with India began with trade. This illustration shows the East India Company's warehouse in Lambeth. The quadrangle was designed by Digby Wyatt (1820-1877). 'Through this range of buildings, which forms a prominent object in the view from Westminster Bridge, looking eastward, passes almost every article of European manufacture or produce which is required by the Government Departments of the Indian empire: the military, marine, public works, medical, trigonometrical surveys, Mint, commissariat, stationery, telegraph, and civil miscellaneous departments.' This list provides an excellent overview of the main functions of imperial government and administration. Through this building 'upwards of 25,000 tons of stores of various descriptions are sent to India annually'. In 1868, the year in which this print was published in the *Illustrated London News*, this figure had been supplemented by an incredible 120,000 packages for the Abyssinian expedition. This was organized from Bombay by the Indian Army under General Sir Charles Napier. Packages included warm clothing, mule pack-saddles, waterproofs, portable cookers, steam ovens, cameras, borehole equipment, mountain batteries, rockets, and all manner of food, as the Anglo-Indian Victorian army conducted expeditionary warfare across oceans and mountain ranges.

JJ East India Company Box 1

TULLOH AND COMPANY

RESPECTFULLY BEG LEAVE TO ACQUAINT THEIR FRIENDS AND THE PUBLIC,

THAT THEY HAVE RECEIVED

THEIR

EXTENSIVE AND CHOICE INVESTMENTS

OF

EUROPE GOODS,

IMPORTED ON THE

HON. COMPANY's SHIPS

GLORY, SARAH CHRISTIANA, ANN, DIANA, AND

NORTHAMPTON;

THE WHOLE LAID IN BY THEIR PARTICULAR INDENT;

WHICH, WITH OTHER PURCHASES,

COMPRISE

A GENERAL AND VALUABLE ASSORTMENT

OF

PRIME ARTICLES,

FROM THE

FIRST TRADESMEN IN LONDON.

Country Orders strictly attended to.

J. GREENWAY AND CO.—HURKARU PRESS.

TULLOH AND CO.

HAVE FOR SALE, ON COMMISSION,

AN EXTENSIVE STOCK

OF

HOUSEHOLD FURNITURE;

(MADE UNDER THE INSPECTION OF EUROPEAN AND NATIVE CABINET-MAKERS)

CONSISTING OF

REAL fine St. Domingo MAHOGANY,
TOON, TEAK, and BLACK WOOD,
DINING TABLES, in Sets, of various dimensions,
BREAKFAST, PEMBROKE, SOFA, and CARD Ditto,
SIDE-BOARDS, with and without Drawers, and Celerets,
CLEOPATRA and other COUCHES,
CHAIRS, of various patterns,
WARDROBES, and large and small CHESTS OF DRAWERS,
CLOTHES HORSES, with and without Boxes, for Shoes, &c.
WASH-HAND STANDS,—a great variety,
COMMODES,—BIDDETS,—FOOT-STOOLS,
LIQUOR CASES and CELERETS,
WRITING TABLES, of various sorts,
BUREAUS and BOOK CASES,
BOOK STANDS, of sizes,
BEDSTEADS, with carved and fluted Pillars, and handsome
    Head-railings; of various sizes,
COUCHES, with Rattan Bottoms,
CHILDREN'S STANDING and SWING COTS,
DITTO CHAIRS, on Stands,
SEA COTS and COUCHES, with and without Drawers,

AND

NUMEROUS OTHER ARTICLES,

AT VERY MODERATE PRICES.

Trade goods in India (*c.* 1810).

Indian goods came to Britain to be sold, and British goods travelled in the opposite direction. Here Tulloh & Company offer a catalogue of European goods recently arrived aboard the East India Company vessels *Glory*, *Sarah Christiana*, *Ann*, *Diana* and *Northampton*. Tulloh & Company were one of the numerous wholesalers importing goods into India and selling them through emporia. The extensive list included household furniture (made of St Domingo mahogany, among other woods) – sideboards, Cleopatra couches, commodes, clothes horses, bureaus, and swing cots; numerous spirits and wines, confectionery, and bottled fruits; saddlery, green baize and Whitney blankets; officers' helmets, hosiery, perfumes and haberdashery; and sporting prints, glassware, 'London-made table cutlery', gunpowder and books.

JJ East India Company Box 1

**'Sale of English goods in Canton',
a picture from the *Illustrated
London News* of 22 May 1858.**

Canton, a port on the Pearl River 75 miles north of
Hong Kong, was the main entry point for European
trade with China. It was the original treaty port,
to which European, primarily British, trade was
confined on the orders of the Chinese government.

But the first opium war, and the Treaty of Nanking
(1842) that brought it to an end, opened four more
ports, and the process of providing access points for
Western trade and influence continued unabated
until the early twentieth century.

JJ Empire & Colonies Folder

COLONIES AND TRADE.

The GOLD MEDAL, being the Premium offered by this Society for conveying from the Iſlands in the South Sea, to any of the Iſlands in the Weſt-Indies ſubject to the Crown of Great Britain, that valuable Plant the BREAD-FRUIT TREE, in a growing State, was this Seſſion adjudged to CAPTAIN WILLIAM BLIGH, of his Majeſty's ſhip Providence, from whom the following Letters and Accounts were received.

SIR,

I CONSIDER it proper that the Society for the Encouragement of Arts, Manufactures, and Commerce, ſhould be made acquainted with the reſult of a voyage to the South Sea, which I have had the honour to execute.

The intention of it was, by his Majeſty's directions, to convey Plants of the Bread-

U   Fruit

The Transactions of the Society for the Encouragement of Arts, Manufactures, and Commerce, vol. xii (1794).

Not only is the typeface arresting in itself, so too is the subject matter – the notification of the Society's Gold Medal award to Captain William Bligh of HMS *Providence* for his work in bringing breadfruit and other specimens from the Pacific to the West Indies (where it was used to feed slaves). There follows a letter written by Bligh from Lambeth on 26 October 1793. This was a fitting accolade for Bligh, whose first Pacific–West Indies breadfruit mission, dispatched in 1789, had resulted in the infamous mutiny aboard his ship HMS *Bounty*. Bligh and the loyal crew members set adrift had endured a remarkable journey to Timor. Earlier in his career he had been Master of HMS *Resolution* during Captain Cook's final (and fatal) mission in 1776. He rose to the rank of vice admiral and served as Governor of New South Wales (1805).

JJ Empire & Colonies Box 1

**'Canada Astride the World's
Trade Routes' (1930s).**

An interesting take on the imperial map of the
world, this Empire Marketing Board promotion
offers the familiar 'red on the map', but with Canada
displacing Britain at its centre. It illustrates the
interconnectedness of a global trading empire, in
which sea routes and merchant ships enabled the
settler colonies to sell their good overseas, most of
them going to Britain to feed its increasingly urban
population, who, in turn, produced manufactured
goods for export.

JJ Emigration Box 1

Gordon & Gotch's *Australian Handbook Shippers' and Importers' Directory and Business Guide 1900 (Incorporating New Zealand, Fiji, and New Guinea).*

This was the thirty-first edition of the guide, 'the standard work of reference on the Australian colonies' (the following year the five Australian colonies came together to form the Commonwealth of Australia). Gordon & Gotch was based on St Bride Street, London, and marketed itself as expert in 'Colonial and Foreign' advertisements and the facilitation of marketing in the colonies.

JJ Empire & Colonies Box 3

Brochure for a West African trade fair (1927).

This publication not only tempts investors but neatly summarizes the standard contemporary view of colonial history that associated British rule with progress and development: the labour of head porters has been replaced by lorries and a road network because of beneficent British rule.

JJ Empire & Colonies Box 4

Illustration from *There is a Market*, an early 1930s' publication of West African Publicity Limited.

The illustration shows a modern grocery shop in Accra, capital of the Gold Coast. It is an image that strikes a familiar note regarding British rule in the colonies, suggesting that it was associated with progress, in this case the development of modern consumer society. *There is a Market* was intended to alert British businessmen to the potential market in British West Africa, and of West African Publicity's marketing reach. 'Never before has such a spirit of Imperial patriotism pervaded in the British commercial community.' The book contained information on subjects such as 'posters and how they are made to appeal', the 'system of distribution and selling' in West Africa, and 'talking to the native by pictures'. The foreword was written by Lord Riddell (1865-1934) shortly before his death. Riddell was a newspaper baron, and had been the government's press liaison officer during the First World War and at the 1921 Washington Naval Disarmament Conference. He was in charge of publications such as the *News of the World*, *Strand Magazine* and *Country Life*, and president of the Royal Free Hospital.

JJ Empire & Colonies Box 5

**A label for India Currie Powder
from the 1850s.** (*above*)

The first recorded curry recipe in Britain appeared
in 1747, and 'currie powder' came to mean a blend
of black pepper, coriander, ginger, turmeric and
other spices. The word is possibly an anglicization
of the Tamil *kari*. The Hindoostanee Coffee House,
Britain's first curry restaurant, was opened in
London in 1810 by the British Bengali businessman
Sake Dean Mahomed. Curry and curry dishes are
staple foods in Britain; coronation chicken, which
uses curry flavouring, was created for the banquet
marking Elizabeth's accession to the throne in
1953, and more recently chicken tikka masala, a
British–Asian hybrid, has been described as Britain's
national dish.

JJ Labels 9 (17b)

**Mogul or real Chetna sauce,
c. 1850s–1870s.** (*right*)

JJ Labels 9 (52a)

112

Arrowroot label *c.* 1820s. (*below*)

Arrowroot was popular in British cooking in the nineteenth century, though its limited nutritional properties led to its demise. It is a powder derived from the wet starch of the rootstock of the herb. It was grown in the West Indies, particularly Jamaica and St Vincent, and was used in children's food and the making of biscuits, jellies, ice-cream, cakes and sauces.

JJ Labels 11 (99g)

Empire matches, *c.* 1890s–1900s. (*above*)

JJ Labels 12 (30a)

Coomassie Burner, *c.* 1880s–1890s. (*below*)

A matchbox label, the name possibly referring to the sacking and burning of Kumasi, the Ashanti capital, during General Sir Garnet Wolseley's expedition to the Gold Coast in 1874.

JJ Labels 12 (34f)

'Pride of Empire' brand
sliced peaches from
Australia, *c.* 1920s–1930s.

JJ Labels 6 (20b)

A label for Penang
pineapples from 1900.

JJ Labels 5 (103)

A bale label for cotton from
the late nineteenth century.
(*left*)

JJ Labels 16 (107b)

A paper bag dating from the mid-1850s from W.M. Henzell's Tea Establishment of Newcastle-on-Tyne.

The company's paper bags carried a series of 'illustrations of natural history', and this one describes the features of African and Asian elephants. It is the very epitome of ephemera.

JJ Paper Bags 1 (6)

ILLUSTRATIONS OF NATURAL HISTORY.

No. 3.—THE ELEPHANT.

THERE are two distinct species of Elephant, the one inhabiting Asia and the other Africa. Whether Asiatic or African they always live in herds, varying greatly in numbers, and are found in or near the deepest forests. Both species are fond of water, and are never found at any great distance from some stream or fountain, although they do make tolerably long journeys to obtain the needful supply. They have a curious capability of laying up a store of water in their interior, somewhat after the fashion of the Camel; and possess the strange accomplishment of drawing the liquid supply from their stomachs by means of their trunks, and scattering it in a shower over their backs in order to cool their heated bodies. When drinking, the Elephant inserts the tip of his trunk into the stream, fills its cavities with water, and then, turning his trunk so as to get the extremity well into his throat, he discharges its contents fairly into his stomach.

From W. M. HENZELL'S
TEA ESTABLISHMENT.
42, West Clayton Street, Newcastle-on-Tyne,
Where First Class Teas, and the Finest Coffees may be had
ALL THE YEAR ROUND.

A series of Colman's Starch adverts using images from the Prince of Wales's tour of India and Ceylon in 1875–76.

The future King Edward VII was a celebrity figure in the British Empire, and his tour gave widespread publicity to Britain's South Asian domains and their attraction as travel destinations. The first picture shows the Prince hunting tiger, while the second picture shows him holding a durbar with Indian princes. In the third, he invests Indian princes with the Star of India. The Prince's tour was widely reported in newspapers such as *The Graphic* and the *Illustrated London News*, both organs keen on covering imperial stories.

JJ Labels 2 (12a), Labels 2 (12b), Labels 2 (12c)

The King Tiger Hunting in India. 1875.

Colman's Starch

The King holds a Durbar, 1876.

Colman's Starch

Our Defenders in South Africa (early 1900s).

This contemporary advertisement is for cough elixir.
It shows Scots Guards and General Sir Redvers
Buller, whose war did not go entirely according
to plan, earning him the nickname Sir 'Reverse'
Buller.

JJ Patent Medicines 2 (47)

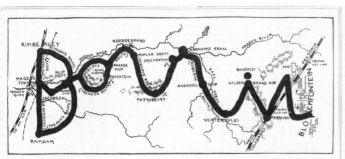

How Lord Roberts spells **BOVRIL**

Careful examination of this Map will show that the route followed by Lord Roberts in his historical march to Kimberley and Bloemfontein has made an indelible imprint of the word Bovril on the face of the Orange Free State.

This extraordinary coincidence is one more proof of the universality of Bovril, which has already figured so conspicuously throughout the South African Campaign.

Whether for the Soldier on the Battlefield, the Patient in the Sick-room, the Cook in the Kitchen, or for those as yet in full health and strength at home,

BOVRIL IS LIQUID LIFE.

March 28, 1900.

'How Lord Roberts spells Bovril' (*c.* 1900).

Lord Roberts (1832–1914) was commander-in-chief in South Africa during the Boer War (1899–1902), and this contemporary advert spells out the product on a map of South Africa charting the progress of British forces. Roberts was ennobled as Lord Roberts of Kandahar, continuing a tradition that saw British civil and military officers choose names associated with their exploits overseas (Napier of Magdala, Mountbatten of Burma, Kitchener of Khartoum, Twining of Godalming and Tanganyika etc.).

JJ Patent Medicines 1 (60a)

An advertisement for Dr Rooke of Scarborough's Oriental Pills and Solar Elixir, 1895, showing a caravan of balsam merchants.

In an advert in the *Sydney Mail* on 24 January 1887 it was claimed that these medicines had the largest stake of any English patent medicine in the world. Introduced in 1836, the medicine was recommended for all cases of pulmonary consumption and as a general health restorer. It was also recommended for wind, indigestion, headaches, 'female complaints' and liver and bowel disorders.

JJ Patent Medicines 12 (3a)

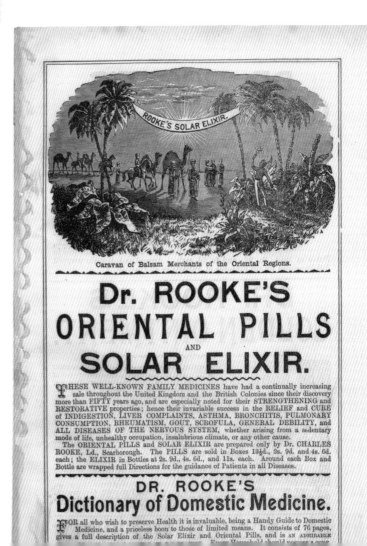

Caravan of Balsam Merchants of the Oriental Regions.

Dr. ROOKE'S ORIENTAL PILLS AND SOLAR ELIXIR.

THESE WELL-KNOWN FAMILY MEDICINES have had a continually increasing sale throughout the United Kingdom and the British Colonies since their discovery more than FIFTY years ago, and are especially noted for their STRENGTHENING and RESTORATIVE properties; hence their invariable success in the RELIEF and CURE of INDIGESTION, LIVER COMPLAINTS, ASTHMA, BRONCHITIS, PULMONARY CONSUMPTION, RHEUMATISM, GOUT, SCROFULA, GENERAL DEBILITY, and ALL DISEASES OF THE NERVOUS SYSTEM, whether arising from a sedentary mode of life, unhealthy occupation, insalubrious climate, or any other cause.

The ORIENTAL PILLS and SOLAR ELIXIR are prepared only by Dr. CHARLES ROOKE, Ld., Scarborough. The PILLS are sold in Boxes 13½d., 2s. 9d. and 4s. 6d. each; the ELIXIR in Bottles at 2s. 9d., 4s. 6d., and 11s. each. Around each Box and Bottle are wrapped full Directions for the guidance of Patients in all Diseases.

DR. ROOKE'S Dictionary of Domestic Medicine.

FOR all who wish to preserve Health it is invaluable, being a Handy Guide to Domestic Medicine, and a priceless boon to those of limited means. It consists of 76 pages, gives a full description of the Solar Elixir and Oriental Pills, and is AN ADMIRABLE

An advertisement for rubber products dating from November 1852.

At the time rubber was known as gutta percha, a version of the Malay *getah perca*, meaning the sap of the percha tree. The genus occurs in Southeast Asia and the Pacific, and from the 1840s the British were using Malayan rubber for such things as telegraph and submarine telegraph wire insulation. As well as gym shoes (long after known as 'gutties' in Scotland) and buckets, the product was used in dentistry and revolutionized numerous sports, including golf. This advert was aimed at people intending to emigrate to the settler colonies and, as the picture indicates, specifically at those in Britain responding to the gold strikes in the colonies of New South Wales (Bathurst) and Victoria (Ballarat) that had occurred in the previous year. The advert commends the advantages of rubber soles and rubber linings for sea chests to protect belongings during the voyage. In the picture the prospective 'digger', destined for Melbourne, contemplates his rubber-lined sea chest, into which he will pack his rubber lifebuoy and gold-panning bowl. On the wall are posters announcing the gold strikes and ships bound for the colony of Victoria, and a ship can be seen at anchor through the window.

JJ Emigration Box 1

TO EMIGRANTS!

The following GUTTA PERCHA ARTICLES will be found of great value to Emigrants, especially such as are proceeding to the

GOLD DIGGINGS.

GUTTA PERCHA LINING FOR BOXES

| BUCKETS. | LIFE BUOYS. | WASHING BOWLS. |
| DRINKING MUGS. | FLASKS. | SYPHONS. |

GUTTA PERCHA TUBING.

| SUCTIONS FOR PUMPS. | CARBOYS FOR GUNPOWDER. |
| JUGS. | MINERS' CAPS. |

SOLES FOR BOOTS AND SHOES.

TO KEEP THE FEET DRY is of the utmost importance to the Emigrant. This may be secured by the use of Gutta Percha Soles, which are perfectly Waterproof, Cheaper, and more Durable than Leather. They can be put on with ease by any one. This cannot be too extensively known amongst Australian Emigrants, as it is now difficult to find a Shoemaker in that country.

Gold Washing Vessels of every variety of shape may be had to order.

Directions to Emigrants for lining Boxes with Gutta Percha Sheet, (so as to preserve the contents from injury by Sea Water), also for putting on Soles of Boots and Shoes, &c., may be had GRATIS on application to any of the Gutta Percha Company's Dealers.

GUTTA PERCHA SOLES.

The Gutta Percha Company have been favoured with the following important testimony from

F. G. AUBIN, ESQ., of the Central London District School,

In which Establishment the Patent Gutta Percha Soles have been in use, for upwards of

Two Years, by EIGHT HUNDRED CHILDREN.

(*Copy.*)   *Weston Hill, Norwood, December 15th, 1851.*

Gentlemen,—In answer to your inquiry, I beg to say that the Gutta Percha Soles have been tried in these Schools for above two years, and I have much pleasure in giving my opinion that for keeping the feet dry, as well as for warmth, durability, and economy, they have proved a most important and invaluable improvement for Children's Shoes and Boots. For all large establishments, particularly of Children, I should recommend their use most strongly.

N. B.—The Company's Illustrated Circulars, containing Instructions to Plumbers for joining Tubes, lining Tanks, &c., will be forwarded (post free) on receipt of three postage stamps.

THE GUTTA PERCHA COMPANY, PATENTEES,
18, WHARF ROAD, CITY ROAD, LONDON.

The British Journal Vol. 2. No. 11 November 1852

**One of a series of booklets
advertising Australian produce
aimed at the British market.**

The cover folds out to reveal several pages of
information on the produce and Australia's market
share within the Empire, and a number of specimen
recipes for delights including 'Australian Sultana
Suet Pudding'. The use of language – 'Australian
eggs for the homeland' – illustrates a commonplace
way of depicting the relationship between Britain,
the homeland or 'motherland', and the settler
colonies – Australia, Canada, Newfoundland, New
Zealand and South Africa. It appealed to ideas of
imperial fraternity, interdependence, and duty
– why buy eggs from a country not in the Empire?
– and strong ties of kith and kin among the
community of 'Greater Britain' or Britain beyond
the seas. The booklets stated bold facts – that, for
example, Australians bought more British goods per
capita than foreigners. Straplines included: 'Empire
Buying results in more work for British factories';
'Empire Buying will help reduce unemployment';
and the slightly confusing 'Empire Buying will keep
your sons and daughters under your own flag'.

JJ Emigration Box 1

A selection of stylish adverts designed by West African Publicity Limited, showing how colonial products were marketed throughout the world (1930s). (*right*)

JJ Empire & Colonies Box 5

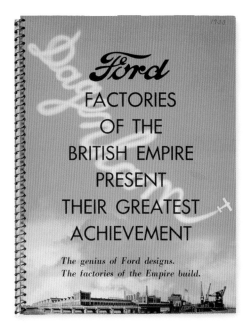

Ford factories of the British Empire present their greatest achievement (1933).

An image from a 1933 Ford brochure, associating its products with British and imperial economic well-being. 'The genius of Ford designs, the factories of the Empire build' went the slogan. In 1931, Ford's factory in Manchester relocated to Dagenham (here spelt out in the trail of the aeroplane). The factory soon became Europe's largest car plant, employing over 40,000 workers.

JJ Motor Cars 2

**'Countries of Empire',
a card game manufactured by
John Jaques of London (1930s).**

Its marketing message is clear from the packet
– 'BUY EMPIRE GOODS FROM HOME AND
OVERSEAS' – and it featured posters published
by the Empire Marketing Board. The Empire
Marketing Board had been set up by the Colonial
Secretary, Leo Amery, in 1926 to promote inter-
imperial trade, and as a partial substitute for
protectionist legislation. In 1933 it was abolished,
having never been particularly successful and
proving increasingly unnecessary when free trade

was finally replaced with a system of imperial
preference (protection) at the 1932 Ottawa
Conference. The Board made over a hundred films
promoting imperial trade, such as *Solid Sunshine*,
about New Zealand butter, *Wheatfields of the
Empire* and *Song of Ceylon*. It was headed by the
well-known documentary film-maker John Grierson
(1898–1972), and became the Crown Film Unit
during the Second World War.
JJ Card Games

Advertisements from the 30 May 1953 edition of the *Investors' Chronicle* published three days before the coronation of Queen Elizabeth II.

To commemorate the occasion, this issue of the weekly magazine was titled *Elizabethan Inheritance* and heralded a new Elizabethan age, indicative of Britain's hope in the post-war years that the Empire would assist its economic recovery, particularly its dollar-earning potential. The *Investors' Chronicle* is one of the oldest magazines in the world, dating from 1860. It began as the *Money Market Review* and in 1914 merged with the *Journal of Finance*. From 1928 it was run by Brendan Bracken, who was also responsible at the time for the *Financial Times*. The magazine still specializes in offering private investors a weekly analysis of the stock market. This advert seeks to tempt investors to consider investing in a new South African venture in the manufacture of iron and steel using the Krupp–Renn process.

The second page provides a good example of the links between London and the colonies. From an office in Malaya House looking out over Trafalgar Square and Nelson's Column, South Africa House and the church of St Martin-in-the-Fields, two men study a map of Malaya, the Empire's biggest dollar-earning territory (at the time in the grips of the conflict known as the Malayan Emergency). Other Empire-related adverts appeared, such as one showcasing the British West Indies and its 'unique industrial opportunities'. The Caribbean, the advertisement stated, offered factory sites close to rail, ship and road transport, abundant supplies of labour and a 'temperate all-year climate, excellent schools, university, modern medical facilities, sports, clubs, modern hotels – everything for gracious living'.

JJ Empire and Colonies Box 1

TRAVEL, COMMUNICATIONS AND THE IMPERIAL NETWORK

As well as being a political entity characterized by overseas settlement, governance and trade, the British Empire was defined by the movement of people, ideas and information. Movement depended on a well-established and always expanding infrastructure of ports, shipping lines, railways, telegraph cables, air routes and airwaves. What held the Empire together and made it a 'real' thing, apart from its constituent territorial units, were the *networks* that connected these territories. Various types of people travelled around the Empire – migrants, soldiers, administrators, seamen, businessmen, touring dignitaries and holidaymakers. The images considered in this chapter relate to the Empire's travel and communications networks, and reflect the fact that many parts of the Empire were acquired *because of* their capacity to facilitate safe communications and intra-imperial trade. Such places included the Cape, Ceylon, Singapore and Labuan.

Travel and communications and the engineering associated with the Empire left a lasting legacy. Bermuda, Bombay, Calcutta, Cape Town, Colombo, Freetown, Gibraltar, Hobart, Hong Kong, Malta, Melbourne, Rangoon, Suez, Sydney and Wellington were either founded or developed because of their proximity to important sea

routes or their possession of natural harbours. Ephemera relating to travel and imperial communications were extensive, and included material published by shipping and airline companies, travel agents and Empire-related clubs and societies. They included new colonial newspapers, pictures of ports and ships, and letterheads depicting scenes such as the General Post Office building in Melbourne.

In the twentieth century, travel became increasingly associated with leisure as it became more affordable. The 'annihilation of distance' was achieved by faster ships and civil airliners, and tourism developed because of this. Shipping lines such as Peninsular and Oriental and Canadian Pacific, which had made their money from carrying the mail and all classes of colonial travellers, were increasingly able to offer 'cruises' for nothing more than the purpose of leisure. Their ships were constructed so that in times of war, as was the British tradition, they could be converted into troopships. Thomas Cook advertised safari holidays, magazines such as *Travel Talk* presented alluring images and stories of exotic lands, and advertisers used the phenomenon of air travel between Croydon and Cape Town to add an air of sophistication and glamour to products such as tobacco.

What was also important for the growth of tourism was the fact that the reputation of the dominions improved as a result of government propaganda. Australia, for example, shed some of its convict associations and New Zealand lost its connection with cannibals. The governments of the settler states became adept at producing literature intended to encourage further settlement from Britain and attract more temporary visitors as tourists. A company called Empire Travel offered 'Round the World' tours, whilst the New Zealand government adopted the slogan 'Playground of the Pacific'. Shipping companies advertised Mediterranean cruises or holidays to attend highland

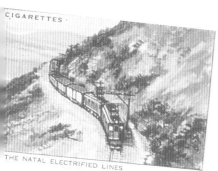

CIGARETTES ·

THE NATAL ELECTRIFIED LINES

gatherings and golfing events in Banff, Canada, as well as log-cabin holidays in the Rockies.

In the twentieth century famous shipping lines and airlines flourished, epitomized by the Cunard liner *Queen Mary* and the flying boat *Canopus*, the first of Imperial Airways' fleet of 'Empire' flying boats built by Short Brothers of Rochester for the burgeoning commercial air market.[1] Liners and merchantmen plied familiar sea routes and stopped at famous ports, whilst passenger aircraft pioneered new air routes, such as Imperial's Trans-Africa route. Port cities, featuring wharves, warehouses, dry docks, hotels, chandleries and bars, developed all over the British world, and new airports were created. The postal system, and from the 1870s the underwater telegraph network, contributed to global communications. In 1909, 3,675,000 lb of mail was despatched to India, and 818,000 lb received from India; 5,022,000 lb went to Canada and Newfoundland, and 1,362,000 lb crossed the Atlantic in the opposite direction.[2] Cheap, fast communications were laying the foundations of modern globalization, and in a variety of interesting ways; cheap travel aboard British-owned liners increased the numbers of Muslims from around the world able to undertake the hajj.

The Allan shipping line of Canada specialized in relocating settlers, a sort of aquatic Pickfords for the 'intending migrant'. Newspapers reported the departure of migration ships, such as the New Zealand Shipping Company's *Eastern Monarch*, as they left Britain and arrived at destinations in the New World. With the opening of the Suez Canal in 1869, P&O were able to offer an 'overland' service from Britain to India via the European continent and the Mediterranean, advertising the service with exotic pictures of the Raj. The Clydeside ports became rich through trade with the Americas and West Indies, and their shipbuilders constructed great liners and warships associated with imperial and national pride. At John Brown's shipyard at Clydebank, for example, the liners *Lusitania*, *Empress of Britain*, *Queen Mary* and *Queen Elizabeth* were all built in the same berth, as was the famous battlecruiser HMS *Hood*. The public were well aware of Britain's shipbuilding prowess and celebrated it, over 250,000 people turning out in Glasgow to see the launch of the *Queen Mary*. The national anthem was played on the newsreel as a stirring English voice announced the birth of another triumph of British shipbuilding, affirming Britain's maritime heritage and supremacy. The great liners of the age, often built specifically for Eastern service, featured interiors intended to rival the Ritz and engines that could generate enough energy to power a town. Before the age of cheap air transport, they were integral to the manner in which people viewed the world. Advertisements for shipping lines featured evocative artwork, similar to that devised by railway companies such as Great Western, romanticizing travel and its associated landscapes.

On land the growth of empire brought new connections in the form of pioneering road and rail networks, as ox wagons gave way to trains, lorries and Land-Rovers. With them went engineering, construction and maintenance expertise, including such things as the Royal East African Automobile Association, formed when the new Mombasa to Nairobi road opened in the mid-1920s. In addition to the spread of the written word brought by the mail and the telegraph, imperial communications and a sense of shared identity were forged by the growth of the imperial print media, from early settler newspapers written in longhand to major national dailies. Titles included the *Labuan Gazette*, the *South Australia News*, the *Melbourne Advertiser* and the *North Atlantic Times*. A sense of imperial community was consciously nurtured by clubs and societies with branches all

over the world, such as the Primrose League, the Royal Colonial
Institute, the Round Table, the Royal Over-Seas League and the
Victoria League. These Empire-minded organizations kept the
Empire before the public and provided networks and services for the
hundreds of thousands of people who travelled in it and worked in it.
Organizations such as the Round Table and the Royal Commonwealth
Society were to the fore in the public presentation of the British
Empire's metamorphosis into the modern-day Commonwealth of
Nations.[3]

**The Allan Line's
1898 handbook.**

'Every intending emigrant to
Canada or the United States
should read this book.' It offered
practical advice on areas in
which to settle, local conditions
and what to pack. Of course,
it was hoped that intending
emigrants would become
customers of the Allan Line and
its fleet of transatlantic vessels,
which sailed from Liverpool to
Quebec, Montreal, Halifax and
Portland, both routes sailing via
Derry (Londonderry).

JJ Emigration Box 2

An illustration of Dunedin, capital of the province of Otago in New Zealand (*c.* 1860).

New port cities took root as Britons settled overseas and the imperial economy developed. As the accompanying article explains, Otago was founded in 1843 by Scottish emigrants who wanted to establish a settlement which reflected the beliefs of the Free Church of Scotland. Less than two decades later, as the picture shows, considerable progress had been made in forging a new settler society. The Otago gold rush peaked in 1863.

JJ Empire & Colonies Box 1

**An engraving of the *Eastern Monarch* from
The Illustrated London News, 9 May 1874.**

Chartered by the New Zealand Shipping Company, the *Eastern Monarch* had been launched that year in Sutherland. Constructed of iron and weighing 1,706 tons, she enjoyed one of the fastest passages yet achieved from Plymouth to New Zealand, taking seventy-one days to reach Lyttelton, the port serving the South Island settlement of Christchurch. The *Lyttelton Times* recorded her arrival on 24 July and reported on the voyage, the ship's interior, and the passengers whom Captain Alexander Douglas had safely delivered. The main cargo consisted of 560 government emigrants about to begin new lives in New Zealand. On the journey they had been entertained with concerts, readings and lectures on New Zealand, Ceylon and India, including stories of tiger hunting. On 5 June there was a special 'Crossing the Line' concert, and the children on board received schooling (as stipulated by the government of New Zealand). The passengers were mainly agricultural labourers and miners, with a sprinkling of carpenters, fitters, machinists, shoemakers and tailors. Most of the 74 single women were 'of the domestic class'. The newspaper reported the spacious 'tween decks accommodation, its saloon of 'a chaste and elegant character', decorated with maple and walnut fretwork panelling relieved by handsome silver mountings. The cabins featured velvet pile couches and handsome Brussels carpets.

JJ Emigration Folder

New overland route to India (*c.*1870s).

A stunning if romanticized image detailing travel
through Continental Europe to the Orient. The
route took the traveller through France to the
port of Brindisi on the heel of the Italian boot and
then eastwards (from 1869) via the newly opened
Suez Canal aboard P&O steamers. The 'gorgeous
scenery & magnificent Cities of the Continent &
the East' were an attraction in themselves. The text
refers to the royal visit of the Duke of Edinburgh,
Queen Victoria's second son. He was at the time an
officer in the Royal Navy, and had some previous
experience visiting parts of the Empire. In 1860
he visited the Cape aboard HMS *Euralyus*, and
as commander of the frigate HMS *Galatea* he
embarked upon a world tour in January 1867.
Leaving from Plymouth he visited Gibraltar, the
Cape, New Zealand and South Australia,escaping
an assassination attempt on a Sydney beach, in
which he sustained a minor gunshot wound. He
arrived in India in December 1869, the first member
of the Royal Family to visit the subcontinent, and
remained there until March 1870.

JJ Empire & Colonies Folder

134

Early transportation in the colonies.

An early-nineteenth-century painting of spans of oxen pulling wagons in South Africa.

JJ Empire & Colonies Box 5

The New Capital to Coast Road: Nairobi to Mombasa (December 1926).

Another example of the transplantation of British institutions to unlikely places: a publication of the Royal East African Automobile Association (note the emblem). The Association was founded in 1919 by Lionel Douglas Galton Fenzi, with the then Governor of Kenya, Sir Edward Northey, as its first chairman. By 1925 the Association had over 2,000 members, indicative of the extent of white settlement in Britain's East African territories. Fenzi had the idea of asking manufacturers to loan cars for trial under African conditions. The Coventry-based Riley company sent him a Riley 12/50, and it was in this vehicle that he pioneered the 300-mile Nairobi to Mombasa route in January 1926, pictures from which are shown in this booklet. He also pioneered the Nairobi–Dar-es-Salam–Nyasaland route, and the Nairobi–Khartoum route, illustrative of the spread of communications and transport networks.

JJ Empire & Colonies Box 4

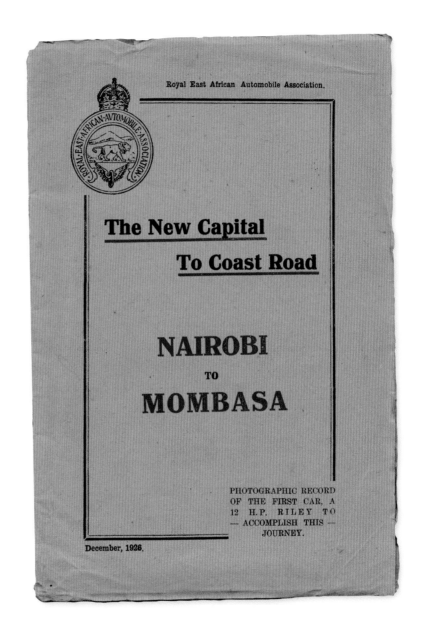

Royal East African Automobile Association.

The New Capital
To Coast Road

NAIROBI
TO
MOMBASA

PHOTOGRAPHIC RECORD OF THE FIRST CAR, A 12 H.P. RILEY TO — ACCOMPLISH THIS — JOURNEY.

December, 1926.

'Empire Railways' series of cards (issued October 1931). (*right*)

W.A. and A.C. Churchman brand cigarette cards from the Imperial Tobacco Company, depicting two railway images from West Africa: 'By the River Niger, Nigerian Railway' and 'Ankobra Bridge, Gold Coast Railway'.

JJ M.L. Horn Collection, Transport album 3

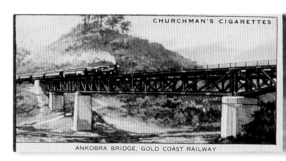

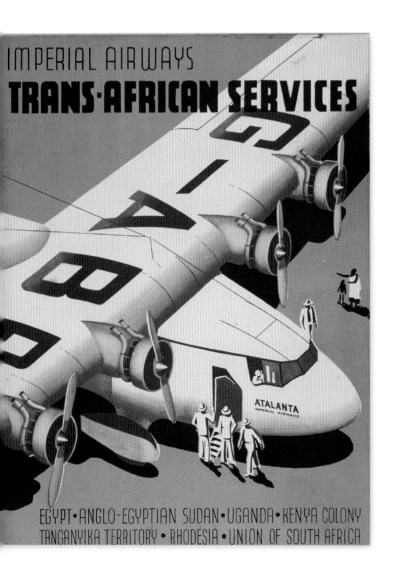

Imperial Airways Trans-Africa Service (July 1932). (*left*)

In 1930 Imperial Airways began its weekly service to South Africa, stopping off on numerous colonies on the way. Its popularity led to its increase to two flights a week in 1935. Imperial Airways entered into talks with the Air Ministry about opening a route from Khartoum to Nigeria; the resultant West Africa service terminated in Kano, and passengers then connected to Lagos by rail. To link the Kano terminus with the Elder Dempster shipping line's dock at Takoradi in the Gold Coast, Elder Colonial Airways was created. A Lagos to Accra route was opened in 1937, and one from Freetown to Bathurst in the following year.

JJ Air 5

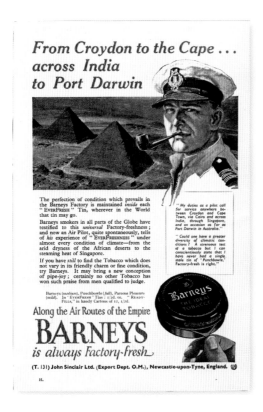

From Croydon to the Cape...
across India to Port Darwin

From Croydon to the Cape…
across India to Port Darwin (1938). (*left*)

Taken from a 1938 copy of *Overseas*, this advert for
Barneys tobacco claims that the product's freshness
is unimpaired by climatic changes. As unlikely as it
may seem today, Croydon was once a hub of imperial
communications. It was the main international
airport for London until Heathrow and Gatwick
were opened. During the First World War an airfield
was built in the area to protect London against
Zeppelin attacks from the Continent, and in 1920
airfields at Beddington and Waddon were combined
to establish Croydon Aerodrome. In the 1920s and
1930s Croydon was the world's busiest airport. It
played a minor role as a base in the Battle of Britain,
though in the post-war world Croydon lost ground
as new airports capable of taking larger modern
aircraft were opened. Croydon finally closed for
business in 1959.

JJ Empire & Colonies Box 1

The new Empire flying boats (1930s).

A cross-sectional diagram of the 'Empire' class
flying boat, manufactured by Short Brothers and
here forming a part of the Imperial Airways fleet.

JJ Air 5

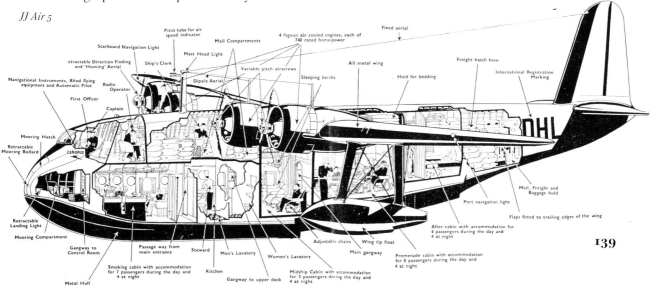

An early colonial newspaper, the *Melbourne Advertiser* of Port Philip. (*below*)

This is the second issue of the first volume, dated 8 January 1838. Items include news of a ship ready to take on board passengers and wool for embarkation to Britain; the loss of a handsome ladies' gold earring between Melbourne and the Salt Water River ford; a cart wanted; 20 pigs and 250 prime cattle for sale; and the freight services of the schooner *Lapwing*.

JJ Empire & Colonies Box 1

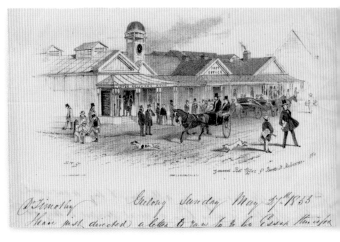

General Post Office, Great Bourke St, Melbourne (1854). (*above*)

A good example of early colonial buildings and the incidental way in which ephemera – in this case a letterhead – conveyed impressions of colonial life. The picture shows the General Post Office on Great Bourke Street, Melbourne in 1854. Bourke Street was created in 1837 when the Hoddle Grid laid down the design of streets and blocks that was to shape what became Melbourne's Central Business District. At the time the Governor of New South Wales, and therefore of the settlement of Melbourne, was Sir Richard Bourke (the Colony of Victoria was not founded until 1851). Bourke Street became one of Melbourne's main thoroughfares, and the GPO shown here soon gave way to a grander building. The street also housed the parliament building and St Patrick's Cathedral. The letter was written in Geelong on 27 May 1855. Note the dress of the pedestrians, and the shoeshine service.

JJ Empire & Colonies Box 1

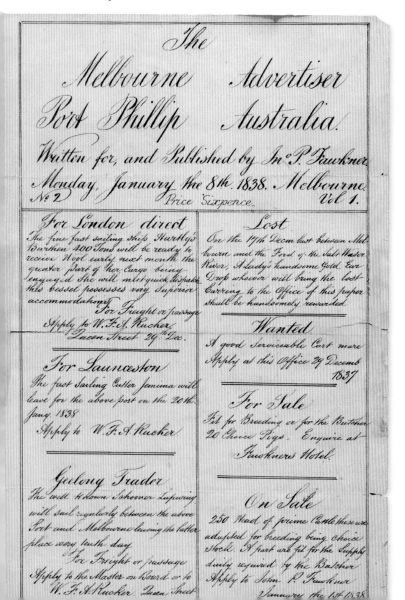

The *South Australian News* from June 1851.

The first news item concerns Australian opposition to the transportation of criminals from Britain; a case, it might be said, of shutting the stable door after the horse had bolted. Of course, many early Australians were free settlers as opposed to convicts. The article considers where the convicts might go if mainland Australia is not to take them. Tasmania? (known then as Van Diemen's Land). The Cape? It is an example of nascent colonial nationalism, the fledgling settler state disputing the policy of the mother country: 'Humanity and justice recommend it: the voice of the population cannot long be disregarded.' Though Adelaide and South Australia were not convict colonies, the point being made was that any part of Australia would soon be 'polluted'. The piece ends with a warning to Westminster: 'Ireland has been the political millstone of every cabinet from times almost immemorial: we must take care that Australia and the Convicts do not form another!'

JJ Empire & Colonies Box 1

THE
South Australian News.

No. 66, New Series.]   JUNE, 1851.   Price 5d. Stamped.

OPPOSITION OF THE AUSTRALIANS TO TRANSPORTATION.

THE unanimity with which the Australian settlers have opposed the transportation of England's criminals to their shores, is one of the most significant facts that can be adduced to prove the impolicy of the system. The convict and the non-convict settlements (with scarcely an exception) have made a most decided stand ; all have been, and are, polluted more or less,— all have determined that their complaints should be loud enough to reach the ears of the public in that older country in which they were formerly resident. But whenever we reflect on this subject, the question arises in all its extent and melancholy importance, " What must be done with the convicts ?" If Australia will not receive them, they must go somewhere else ; if Van Diemen's Land and the Cape will not allow them to land, they must be sent to Moreton Bay and Swan River. But these two settlements will, probably, see fit to open a "Schon" emigration : what export do these hear out ?

The only feasible alternative, seems to be to keep them in this country, where our means of reformation and control are so ample as to prevent the majority, if not all, of the evils which are so justly the cause of complaint in the southern colonies. To this point the matter must come : humanity and justice alike recommend it : the voice of the population in Australia and Van Diemen's Land cannot long be disregarded, nor the welfare of those provinces sacrificed for a financial consideration.

Though South Australia is happily preserved by an Act of Parliament from the curse of being made a *convict* settlement, yet it indirectly shares in the baneful results of a criminal population in the neighbouring colonies. Emancipated convicts do not unfrequently visit Adelaide, where their contaminating influence becomes painfully visible in the cases brought before the police courts. And here, too, public feeling is strongly and universally opposed to transportation ; indeed, so much so, that should the colony's rights be at any time invaded, we may confidently expect a similar line of conduct to that pursued by the Cape colonists in the case of the ship *Neptune*.

Something, however, must be speedily done. The attention of Parliament has lately been pointedly called to the whole question of transportation, and, with a little more agitation, the government will be obliged to propose some scheme as a substitute. Ireland has been the political millstone of every cabinet from times almost immemorial : we must take care that Australia and the Convicts do not form another !

THE AUSTRALIAN MINING COMPANY'S MEETINGS.

THIS unfortunate Company has lately had two Meetings, the former of which is elsewhere fully reported, while the latter, held on the 29th ulto., was merely for the purpose of adopting the recommendations of the Committee of Investigation. All the old directors but two have resigned, so that a meeting will soon be convened to elect a new board, the fees payable to which will not, in future, exceed 200*l.* per annum. The state of the Company is so unsatisfactory that nothing but the most prompt and energetic measures can at all retrieve its affairs. A call of 1*l.* per

share has been made, the whole of which is required to liquidate various debts. Not very long ago the shares were at par—now, alas ! they are quoted at from ten to fifteen shillings—4*l.* having been paid. The Adelaide Committee is to be abolished—a step certainly in the right direction.

SUMMARY OF INTELLIGENCE FROM THE COLONY.

By the Overland Mail we have received news to the 17th February. Business seems to have been rather flat ; large imports having been made, while the arrival of immigrants was less than usual. The greater part of the season's wool had been shipped, as well as large quantities of copper and copper ore. All these commodities will, we believe, realise a very fair price in this market. Wheat had risen to 4s. 3d. per bushel, so that there was little probability of any considerable shipments of it being made to this country ; the miserable results of last year's consignments having proved to the Adelaide merchants that they must not look to the English market for profitable returns. The census taken on the 1st January last, exhibited a total population of 63,000 souls, 34,975 of whom were males, and 29,664 females, to which were added 361 for omissions and persons travelling. The quantity of surveyed land at the same period, purchased and unpurchased, comprised 620,266 acres ; 240,195 being open for sale. All these commodities therefore need be under no fear, as to the extent of land upon which they may settle ; for independently of these 240,195 acres, there are districts yet unvisited by the Surveyor-General and his staff.

The Return which appears in another column of Imports and Exports of the province for the year 1850, shows a rather unusual result for South Australia. The imports were valued at £819,784 12s., while the exports amounted to £545,039 14s. leaving a balance against the colony of £274,744 18s. In 1849, the former were £570,537, the latter £4,455 12s. We subjoin a list of the principal articles, with their estimated value, exported in each of these years :—

1850				1849		
Copper Ore	8,784 tons	£179,316		9,999 tons	....	£182,807
Copper	44,591 cwt.	174,574	"	8,656 cwt.	....	33,872
Wool	3,266,077 lbs.	131,730	"	2,593,912 lbs.	....	107,921
Tallow	3,860 cwt.	5,509	"	5,882 cwt.	....	9,085
Wheat	13,455 qrs.	20,957	"	10,240 qrs.	....	15,469
Flour	1,560 tons	36,573	"	1488 tons	....	16,795
		£528,659				£365,580

It is obvious, however, that the prosperity of a colony does not depend upon the imports and exports balancing each other ; for the amount of each may be so limited in relation to the population, that it would prove the existence of distress, rather than of prosperity. In regard to the imports into the province during last year, it is worthy of mention, that there was a considerable quantity of mining and other machinery sent thither, the expensiveness of which will in some slight degree account for the large amount of imports, while the benefits that will arise from the use of the machinery have not yet had time to develope themselves. But leaving this circumstance out of the question, we may fairly conclude that the South Australians must be in a pretty sound state, when independently of the import of articles used in trade and commerce, they can consume so large a quantity of goods, and at the same time export produce amounting to the value of £545,000, being at the rate of £9 per head of the population.

Political matters were engrossing much public attention ; the "South Australian Gazette" of the 13th February, remarking that " four political meetings of one sort or another per diem, seems to be about the average of the past week in Adelaide and its environs." The Act for the New Constitution was proclaimed on the 20th January, and it was expected that on the 18th February, the Council would fix the Electoral Districts. Pending this necessary preliminary, the colonists were busy nominating candidates for the various districts into which the province would be divided. The reports of the Election meetings take up so much of the attention of the press, that little else is referred to : a good deal of irrelevant matter was of course brought forward, and the paper before alluded to, curtly says, " we have no space to allude to any more of these meetings, which in spite of the indefinite quantity of nonsense

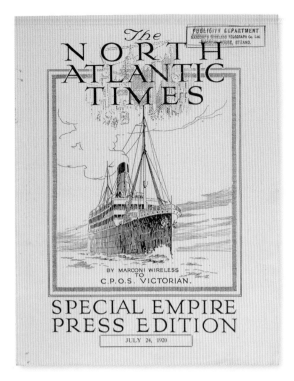

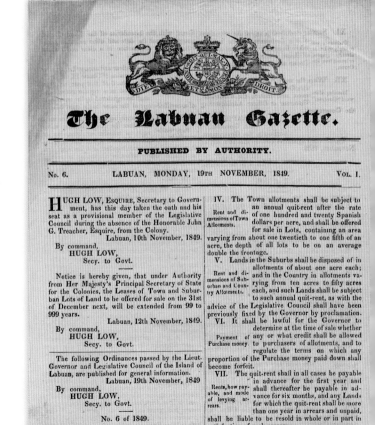

The *Labuan Gazette* of 19 November 1849. (*below*)

This image illustrates the growth of the media even in colonial outposts and the spread of British ways of conducting administrative business and disposing of land. Labuan (from the Malay word for anchorage), situated on the coast of Borneo, had been taken at the suggestion of the Admiralty in order to provide a way station on the long haul between Singapore and the growing Australasian settlements. It was used as a base for anti-piracy activities and also became a coaling station and a cable and wireless station. It was ceded to Britain by the Sultan of Brunei in 1846, and became a Crown colony in 1848.

JJ Emigration Box 1

The *North Atlantic Times* 'Special Empire Press Edition' from 24 July 1920. (*above*)

Published by Canadian Pacific and Marconi, this was a pioneering at-sea publication made possible by newly developed telegraph technology. It provided a news service for passengers aboard transatlantic Canadian Pacific liners. Canadian Pacific Ocean Services gave permission for the installation of a telegraphy set aboard the liner *Victorian*. The Marconi station at Poldhu transmitted news, and the Chelmsford transmitter broadcast music. On board the ship were delegates for the Imperial Press Union conference. *The North Atlantic Times* was published every morning and evening during the voyage and was edited by Arthur Burrows, head of publicity at Marconi. Over 300 miles from the Canadian shore, the leader of the delegation, Lord Burnham, was able to converse with the premier of Newfoundland.

JJ Shipping 19

A pamphlet detailing the aims of the Round Table movement, dating from early 1918.

The movement originated with the men responsible for implementing the post-Boer War federation of South Africa. The federal idea, it was believed, should be translated to the entire Empire, so that a meaningful and politically cohesive unit could be formed. As the pamphlet states, 'permanent unity would secure lasting peace among more than a quarter of the whole human race', a classic rendition of the belief that the British Empire was synonymous with peace and progress.

JJ Empire & Colonies Box 1

Home and Overseas, **the journal of the Royal Over-Seas League founded in 1910.**

This issue dates from 1937, the year in which the club's premises in St James's Street, 400 yards from Buckingham Palace, were expanded. Known as the Empire Wing, the extension featured a Hall of India banqueting room. This issue contained Evelyn Wrench's regular column 'Overseas: A Link of Empire', and articles such as 'The Empire Flying Boats'.

JJ Empire & Colonies Box 1

THE
VICTORIA
LEAGUE

Stands for the FAMILY Concept of Commonwealth and E[m]

No. 1.   Nov. 1903.   2d.

British
and Colonial
Traveller.

Every Traveller

should include a supply of Bovril in his kit—he will enjoy
and appreciate its stimulus and nourishment when in a
"tight place" where ordinary meals are out of immediate
reach. Bovril contains the albumen and fibrine—the best
properties of the beef. It is this fact—together with its
absolute purity—that commends Bovril to Physicians, Scientists,
Travellers, Athletes, etc., in all civilized countries.

BOVRIL

**The Victoria League 'stands for the FAMILY
concept of Commonwealth and Empire'.**
(*above*)

The League grew out of dismay among some
women in 1901 about fighting and discord in South
Africa, and a meeting of women at 10 Downing
Street established the League, named after the
late Queen, soon after. It has been dedicated to
intra-Commonwealth friendship and links ever
since, making particular efforts, to this day, to
host Commonwealth citizens, particularly students
visiting Britain. It is non-political, and its work
has included tending war graves and sending food
parcels during conflict. This booklet dates from the
Society's jubilee year, 1951.

JJ Empire & Colonies Box 1

***British and Colonial Traveller*,
launched in November 1903.**

In his introduction the editor states that the
magazine's intention was to 'present to the general
public – but more especially to travellers to and
from the British Isles – a monthly magazine of
interest and amusement'. It was to be found 'in
many of the leading clubs and hotels throughout the
English-speaking world'.

JJ Travel Box

The first edition of Sir Clements Markham's travel magazine, issued on New Year's Day 1909.

The cover captures a typical 'allure of the desert/ Empty Quarter' image. Sir Clements Markham (1830-1916) was a geographer, explorer and writer. He served as secretary and as president of the Royal Geographical Society, that quintessentially Victorian and imperial creation which embodied the desire to discover, explore and name. Whether consciously intended or not, the work of the RGS was both instigator and handmaiden of imperial expansion and fuelled public interest in peoples and landscapes 'over there'. As a young naval officer Markham had taken part in HMS *Assistance*'s search for the lost Arctic expedition of Sir John Franklin. He accompanied General Sir Robert Napier's military expedition to Abyssinia in 1868. He was geographer to the India Office, and was involved in the transplantation of cinchona, the plant from which quinine is derived, from Peru to India. Among other things, he organized the 1901-04 National Arctic Expedition. Markham gave his name to a mountain, a river and a college – in Antarctica, Papua New Guinea and Peru, respectively.

JJ Prospectuses of Journals 50 (31)

TRAVEL · & EXPLORATION

Prospectus OF A NEW MONTHLY MAGAZINE Devoted to Travel in all its aspects.

FULLY ILLUSTRATED WITH PHOTOGRAPHS. SOUND IN MATTER. POPULAR IN FORM.

FOR FULL DETAILS SEE WITHIN. *For List of Contributors see Back Pages of Cover.*

FIRST NUMBER, JAN. 1, 1909.

Travel Talk. (*below*)

A new travel and sports magazine launched in 1909, and aimed at 'the Greater Traveller' – that is, the one who ventured beyond relatively well known parts of the world. Thus, as the foreword explains, 'in dealing with Africa, articles descriptive of those half-known districts washed by the Niger, the Congo, or the Zambesi will appeal to us more than paragraphs on the tourist season in Tangiers'. Articles in this first issue included 'A Woman Alone in Savage Africa', 'Travel in the Air' and 'Sir Richard Burton, the World's Greatest Explorer'. Thus the magazine contained the standard fare for such publications, and the cover illustration shows a very common reflection of the assumed subservience of non-whites and superiority of whites.

JJ Travel Box

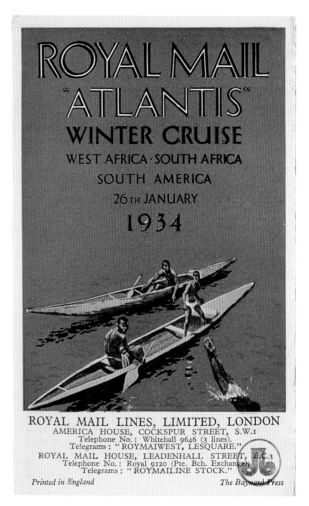

Royal Mail *Atlantis* winter cruise (26 January 1934). (*above*)

Taking you to exotic locations in West Africa, South Africa, and South America.

JJ Baynard Press 4

Timetable for the 1932 Mediterranean cruise of *Empress of Australia*, another Canadian Pacific liner. (*right*)

Built as SS *Tirpitz* in 1913 for the Hamburg–America line, she was taken as war reparation in 1919 and renamed. She served for two years with P&O before joining the Canadian Pacific fleet in 1922. The 21,500-ton ship rescued survivors from the Great Kanto earthquake in Japan in 1923, and in 1927 took the Prince of Wales to Canada for the dominion's diamond jubilee celebrations. In 1929 Winston Churchill, his son Randolph and his brother Jack travelled on the ship for a three-month tour of Canada and America. In 1939 she was the Royal Yacht for the King and Queen's visit to Canada, and during the Second World War and the Korean War was employed as a troopship.

JJ Shipping Lines Box 5

Brochure for the Canadian Pacific liner *Empress of Britain* early 1930s. (*left*)

Built between 1928 and 1931, this 42,000-ton ship was the largest and fastest vessel sailing between Britain and Canada. She was specifically designed to tempt customers away from the Southampton to New York route, and to try a transatlantic route that terminated at Halifax in Nova Scotia. When war broke out in 1939 she was requisitioned as a troopship. In late October 1940 she was spotted off the west coast of Ireland by a Focke-Wulf C200 Condor, which successfully bombed and immobilized her. Some 623 passengers and crew were taken off, and she was taken under tow. But she was torpedoed by *U-32* and sunk, the largest ship to fall victim to submarines during the war.

JJ Shipping Lines Box 5

Cruise from Liverpool and Avonmouth to the West Indies, *Duchess of Atholl*, 1930.

A Canadian Pacific liner weighing over 20,000 tons, she was sunk by *U-178* 200 miles east-north-east of Ascension on 10 October 1942, en route from Durban and Cape Town to Britain. Of 832 passengers and crew, all but 5 survived.

JJ Shipping Lines Box 4

A Thomas Cook safari advertisement (1920s–30s). (*right*)

JJ Exploration Box

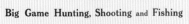

Big Game Hunting, Shooting and Fishing

To the experience of travel may be added the excitement of Big Game Hunting and the fascination of Big Game photography, either in Africa, India, Malay, Indo-China, New Zealand, Canada, or elsewhere. All arrangements can be made in advance as to licences, transportation, experienced white hunters, camp equipment, stores, trackers and servants.

FOR FULL PARTICULARS CONSULT "SHOOTING AND FISHING DEPARTMENT"

THOS. COOK & SON, LTD.
In Co-operation with WAGONS-LITS CO.
HEAD OFFICE: BERKELEY ST., LONDON, W.1.

CEYLON

The Supremely Beautiful Island

Full information from the Trade Commissioner (Room 52), 28 Cockspur Street, S.W.1

Printed by Love & Malcomson Ltd., Redhill, Surrey, for The Trident Magazine, the P. & O. and its Associated Companies in the United Kingdom, New Zealand, Australia and Canada

An evocative advertisement from the April 1939 edition of *The Trident*.

The Trident: A Magazine of the Sea, Travel, History, and Geography contained lavish adverts, including one for the first cruise of the newly refitted P&O liner *Viceroy of India*; for the British Indian Steam Navigation Company, offering services from Europe to India and East Africa, and regional connections to Iraq, Iran, Rangoon, Malaya, Burma, China and Japan; and for Railways of East Africa, inviting readers to 'come to the land of vivid contrasts'. Articles and features included 'Cleopatra's Needle at Sea', 'Gate of the Empire's Sea Road', 'New Zealand's Centennial Celebrations', 'Street Scenes in Malaya', 'Naval Heraldry' and 'Building a Liner'.

JJ Travel Box

EMPIRE, LEISURE
AND POPULAR CULTURE

Imperial ideas were embedded in British popular culture, even if knowledge and understanding were neither uniform nor erudite. What was 'imperial' and what simply 'foreign' or 'exotic' was not distinctly marked in popular understanding. Whilst literature relating to tourism, for example, often had an imperial theme or one that played on shared awareness of stereotypes about non-European people, it often had nothing to do with empire, featuring instead, perhaps, the Alps or the Riviera. Highlighting the imperial theme in popular culture should not blind us to the fact that this was just one theme, and that there were others that were just as powerful. Furthermore, imperial themes were sometimes inextricably bound to other cultural themes, such as racial pride, patriotism, navalism, militarism and even Christianity. Many cultural references to empire had no intentional message and were, as far as these things ever can be, 'innocent'. Thus some manufacturers used imperial images to advertise their wares simply because they liked them; similarly, many people viewed these images without giving them a second thought. Nevertheless, we must acknowledge the more damaging impact, and possible intent, of some advertisements. Some soap advertisements have become notorious for their racial stereotyping and this has been interpreted as a means of enhancing colonial control; images of smiling Africans washing themselves white shaped British perceptions both of themselves and of their Empire, configuring '"whites" as powerful, responsible, improving and regulating in relation to "black" subjects'.[1]

Having marked out these caveats, there is little doubt that imperial and wider world imagery was frequently encountered by the British public and helped shape the way that people viewed Britain and its place in the world. This was always a more striking aspect of popular imperialism than detailed knowledge of imperial territories per se, and much of it was communicated by a 'boom in ephemera and "free gifts"'.[2] This is vital context because a sense of Britishness and of Britain's mission in the world was perhaps the most significant impact of the vast amount of imperial and wider world imagery put before the public. The reason for the prevalence of imperial and wider world images in British popular culture had a lot to do with its relatively *uncontroversial* nature. Advertisers, children's literature publishers and missionary societies all 'found the imperial adventure tradition socially and politically acceptable, as well as immensely popular'.[3]

Themes relating to empire and the wider world were manifest in many forms, from prints of epic art to penny-dreadful stories, posters and illustrated newspapers, leaflets, schoolboy comics, music-hall productions, textbooks and cricket – an imperial game whose demise (from the point of view of the performance of the England team) seemed to match the country's decline in the decolonization years.[4] The cinema and the radio were important in the twentieth century, though the boom in popular cultural forms had been caused initially by nineteenth-century phenomena such as the advent of cheap printing and wider public literacy.[5] This chapter considers the proliferation of imperial images encountered in popular cultural items, everyday objects and public events, including calendars, sheet music, plays, music-hall songs and board games.

'Playing empire' in one form or another fired the imaginations of generations of children.[6] 'Cowboys and Indians' was a quintessentially colonial game. Toy soldiers had their 'fuzzy-wuzzy' enemies to fight against as well as their Napoleonic foes (the term 'fuzzy-wuzzy' was sometimes used generically to describe Africans, particularly African soldiers, and derived from British encounters with soldiers from a particular north-east African community who sported very large, matted hair styles; it was popularized by Kipling's poem of the same name relating to fighting in the Sudan). Feats of exploration inspired games manufacturers to produce board games, as did traditional tales of pirates and treasure ('Pirate and Traveller' game) and technological advances such as the global postal service ('The Overland Mail Route' game). Military endeavour was a perennial subject for those seeking to part children from their pocket money, games including 'Raising Kitchener's Army' and 'The Boer War Game'. Other manufacturers devised dice-roll games such as Betts' mid-1850s' 'A Tour of Britain's Overseas and Foreign Possessions'. Bright imperial images abounded, as did racial clichés and didactic messages about the beneficence of British rule.

Comics and novels followed this trend. In the settler colonies and places such as the West Indies, British literature was held up as a benchmark, whilst indigenous and settler art and expression were often looked down upon or disparaged. *Cole's First Book for Little Australians* was a classic of Victorian education, with a few touches of local colour, whilst the *Empire Annual for Australian Boys* contained articles designed for the British market with a selection specific to the Antipodes (such as 'In the Great Australian Desert').

Comics and juvenile journals such as *C.B. Fry's Magazine* and *The Captain* developed the imperial adventure tradition and peddled the imperialist creed, as did adult equivalents such as the *Wide World Magazine*. In these publications 'character', athleticism, adventure, sport, science, the great outdoors and progress met a value system based upon healthy patriotism, duty, loyalty and the determination to 'right wrongs'. Art, much of it disseminated to the public through commercially marketed prints, often reflected imperial and patriotic themes, as produced by artists such as Richard Caton Woodville (1856-1927) and Lady Elizabeth Butler (1846-1933).

Popular music contained imperial themes and messages, in the background and sometimes very much in the foreground. Edward Elgar was associated with imperial patriotism, perhaps best epitomized by the 'Coronation March' (1911), 'The Crown of India' (1912) and the 'Empire March' (1924). But there were many other musical forays with an imperial flavour. Particular imperial events, such as the Indian Mutiny or the death of military 'heroes' in colonial wars, stirred songwriters and composers. The 'Arctic Expedition Galop' and the 'Farewell to England' waltz were representative titles, whilst in a later age Noël Coward sang of a cosmopolitan colonial world and confirmed numerous national and racial stereotypes whilst gently poking fun at both the British and the 'amusing' people over whom they ruled. Significant national events and themes such as the slave trade and the South Sea Bubble were also reflected in music and song. A Christmas 1897 souvenir showed a verse from 'God Save the Queen' set to music and translated into fifty of the languages spoken in the Empire.

Plays performed on the stage often had an imperial flavour, though imperial or wider world elements were more often present in the form of *unspoken* assumptions reflecting a general societal understanding of the world and Britain's place in it. Thus non-Europeans could variously, and in an uncontroversial manner, be portrayed as comical, feckless, devious or stupid without raising many eyebrows. Moments of patriotic display, such as jubilees and coronations, inevitably spawned a range of plays and songs with fittingly imperial tones celebrating, perhaps, the unity of the 'nations' that made up the British Isles as well as the supposed unity of the races that made up Britain's overseas empire. The beneficence of the monarch's rule and the loyalty of her subjects was another theme. Plays along these lines included Her Majesty's Theatre's 'Under One Flag', and 'Carnac Sahib' at the Elephant and Castle, in which India, Indians and the British in India were presented in a stereotypical fashion.

National cultural events associated with empire included Empire Day, instituted in 1902 on Queen Victoria's birthday. The idea of the event was to remind children that they were part of the British Empire and to encourage them to think of their fellow 'sons and daughters' of the British Empire in the settler colonies across the seas. It was recognized as an official event in 1916, renamed British Commonwealth Day in 1958 and, signalling the speed of decolonization, Commonwealth Day in 1966. Empire Day celebrations featured the saluting of the flag and pageants in which children dressed as national symbols and imperial 'heroes'. There were plenty of other events and organizations that contributed to imperial patriotism and left a distinct footprint in terms of ephemera, including the Empire Youth Movement, the Boy Scouts and Girl Guides ('scout' and 'guide' being names given to paramilitary forces on the fringes of empire) and the Kipling Society.

Images of empire and the wider world had a profound impact on British culture. 'The persistence of exotic imagery in everyday consumer settings affirmed them, and translated the harsh aspects

of imperial dominance into picturesque and pleasing forms. The consumability of empire in foods, entertainment, political gatherings or advertising involved both pleasure and practical need, and cultural meanings as well as monetary calculations.[7] One might discern vestiges of this in cultural representations and advertising to this day – in tea advertisements, for example, that show smiling, happy 'native' women picking tea leaves on estates and then smiling, happy British families savouring the beverage in their cosy living rooms. Overlaid with a 'fair trade' message, this comfortably associates consumers with apparently contented and fairly treated 'Third World' producers. We can all sleep easy.

Circassian Persian.   Group of Chinese.   Tartar. Saracen.
Lady.

Indian.   Mexican.   Woman of Otaheite   Esquimaux and Dog. Caribean Chief.
Dancing.

Russian.   Turk.   Swedish Lady. Highlander. Dutch. Spanish. English.

Moor.   Egyptian.   Slave of the   Planter. Boa Constrictor
Spynx and Pyramids   Gold Coast.   and Stag.

23   ASHANTEE.

AFFRICANA.

Representations of the 'four quarters of the globe', *c.* 1820s–1830s. (*left*)

A good example of the manner in which 'wider world' themes and representations often subsumed those relating more specifically to 'empire'. This is an early-nineteenth-century portrayal of different peoples of the world, close to home – in Scotland and other parts of Europe such as Scandinavia – and farther afield. Parts of the expanding Empire are represented – such as territories in West Africa, North America, and the Caribbean – as well as places such as Russia, China, Persia and the Magreb, and parts of the world with which people were familiar before the Empire became so extensive – such as Egypt and the lands of 'Moors' and 'Saracens'. Note the depiction of animals such as snakes and stags, and the disturbing representation of a planter flogging a slave.

JJ Trade in Prints and Scraps 5 (29)

Ashantee (1820–30)

(*left*)

Britain was engaged with the peoples of West Africa through the slave trade, and from the eighteenth century through the work of missionaries as well as traders in palm oil products. The Ashanti were a people of the territory that was to become the Gold Coast colony (modern-day Ghana), and the British went to war with the kingdom in the 1870s, sacking the capital Kumasi.

JJ Miniature Theatre 5 (34c)

A charming calendar from 1938 produced in Lagos by the Church Missionary Society Bookshop.

(*right*)

The sketches are by Captain R.R. Oakley and the sonnets by C.A. Woodhouse, a former colonial administrator in the Northern Provinces.

JJ Empire & Colonies Box 4

Madame Tussaud & Sons' Exhibition (1841).

A December 1841 playbill depicting
Commissioner Lin, 'the author of the China war,
the destroyer of £2.5 million of British property
and his small-footed wife, the first of the kind
ever exhibited in this country ... giving a perfect
idea of the countenance, costume, and ornament
of those singular people'. This is an example
of the manner in which events in distant lands
– and foreign people – were served up for the
information and entertainment of the British
public, and how a very pro-British gloss was
put on acts of imperial aggression. In this case,
the First Opium War is squarely blamed on
Lin Zexu (1785-1850), a mandarin of the Qing
dynasty who opposed Britain's prosecution of
the opium trade because of the physical and
moral debilitation it caused to Chinese people.
For resisting the British in this way, he has
subsequently been seen as a national hero.
His actions at the time of the Opium Wars,
when he destroyed British opium, illustrated
the fascinating gulf in perception and power
between the declining Chinese empire and the
parvenu industrialists from Britain. Whilst
Lin wrote condescendingly to Queen Victoria
asking that her people desist from interfering
with the affairs of distant China, British trade
and military interests wielded power on the
ground that the Chinese were simply unable to
resist.

JJ Waxworks 1 (55)

MADAME TUSSAUD & SONS' EXHIBITION,
BAZAAR, BAKER STREET, PORTMAN SQUARE.

The Author of the Chinese War!

The Destroyer of £2,500,000, of British property, and his Small Footed Wife,
the only Figures of the kind ever Exhibited in this Country.

COMMISSIONER LIN,
And his Favourite Consort,

Modelled from Life, by the Celebrated LAMB-QUA, of Canton, with the Magnificent Dresses actually worn by them, and the various Ornaments, &c.

Giving a perfect idea of the *Countenance, Costume, and Ornaments* of those singular people the Chinese, of whom so little is known; lately brought to this Country by a Gentleman, a resident of Canton Eighteen Years, and to whom reference can be given.

Selections from the Public Prints.

MADAME TUSSAUD'S EXHIBITION.—This very amusing collection of the portraits in wax, or composition, of so many of the remarkable personages, both male and female, of the past, as well as the present time, has just been rendered more attractive by the addition of two figures, the one representing the notorious Commissioner Lin, and the other his favourite wife. The figures are as large as life, and were modelled from life by an artist of the name of Lamb-Qua, of the city of Canton, where his reputation is exceedingly high. These effigies of the Chinese functionary and his consort are clothed in the actual dresses formerly worn by the originals, and decorated with some very costly ornaments of gold of Chinese manufacture, and with watches of English manufacture, which were once in the possession of the originals. The robes, which are of silk of the richest texture are embroidered

The figures themselves are really an admirable work of art, and from the circumstances under which they were modelled, and the known accuracy of Chinese artists of all sorts, we should imagine the likenesses to be of good authority. The commissioner has a very excellent face, quite sensible, and gentlemanly; and the lady does great credit to his judgment. The dresses, which are described as being those worn by the parties themselves at the court of Pekin, are only just less beautiful. The second portrait — a portrait, which has been added, is a ... of the Princess Royal, in her cot; the latter is a fac-simile of the original at the Palace; whether her Royal Highness is represented with equal fidelity, we cannot exactly say, but there certainly is a very near resemblance in her features to the royal family.—*Morn. Chronicle.*

MADAME TUSSAUD'S EXHIBITION.—It cannot be said

Australian convict ships opened to the public (1890s).

A catalogue and guide for a convict ship that had become a visitor attraction for commoners and royals alike. In the guide we are told that the ship *Success*, launched in India in 1790, had been chartered by the Admiralty in 1829 and became the pioneer vessel in West Australian waters. When founding the Swan River Colony in 1829 (which became the colony of Western Australia in 1832), *Success*'s captain, James Stirling, named the capital Perth after the then Secretary of State for the Colonies, Sir George Murray, who had been born in Perth and was MP for Perthshire. Or so the brochure claims. It is, however, an interesting example of invented history. *Success* had in fact been launched in Burma in 1840, initially trading around India before London owners put her on the emigration run to Australia. In the 1850s she became a prison hulk in Australia, though changed career again in 1890 when she was bought by a group of entrepreneurs. They launched her as a museum ship intended to travel the world as a floating exhibit about the trials of transportation. In doing so they amalgamated her history with that of other ships, notably HMS *Success*, an altogether different vessel that had indeed been present at the founding of Western Australia in 1829, captained by the said James Stirling. The 'new' *Success* toured Australian ports with varying degrees of success, before sailing for England where she appeared at Dungeness in 1894 (the visit from which this brochure dates). In 1912 she went to America, where she slowly disintegrated, though she survived long enough to make a swansong appearance at the 1933 Chicago World Fair.

JJ Empire & Colonies Box 1

159

Empire Day (early twentieth century).

Celebrated annually on 24 May, the anniversary of Queen Victoria's birthday was commemorated as 'Empire Day' and was the occasion for street parties and school pageants. Here we see three postcards, one showing 2,600 Sheffield schoolboys spelling out the words 'God Save the King', another showing the different peoples of the Empire surrounding a monument to the late Queen, with a picture of her son and successor, Edward VII, and a stirring patriotic message ('One King, One Flag, One Fleet, One Empire'); the last depicts the settler colonies according to their associated animal mascots.

JJ John Fraser Collection: Propaganda: GB (3)

KANGAROO.

k

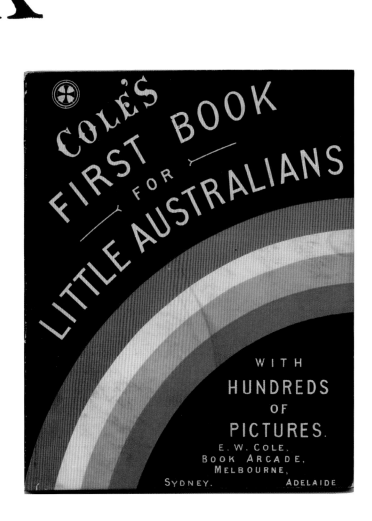

Cover and page detail from Cole's
***First Book for Little Australians, c.* 1908.**

Edward William Cole (1832–1918) was a founding
father of Australian children's literature. He was
born in Kent and ran away to London as a youngster.
In 1850 he emigrated to Cape Colony, and two years
later arrived in Victoria. He set up his famous Book
Arcade in Melbourne, soon moving to premises near
the Post Office on Bourke Street.

JJ Empire & Colonies Box 3

**The first edition of *Wide World*
magazine, April 1898.** (*left*)

*The Wide World: The True Adventure Magazine
for Men* was published between 1898 and 1965.
'Truth is stranger than fiction' was its strapline.
From its front cover, usually dominated by a
scene of adventure or war in distant lands, this
popular comic-cum-magazine looked much like a
boys' magazine, but it was in fact aimed at adults.
Subject matter included the romance of sea hunting
(evincing a peculiarly dated view of the 'romantic');
travel to the North Pole; 'Battle Royal with a Tiger';
a new route to the Klondike goldfield; 'queer sights
in China'; 'the cruise of the slaver *Carl*'; and 'down
the Perak River'.

JJ Prospectuses of Journals 52 (31a)

**An image from The Captain, C.B. Fry's short-
lived magazine for boys (*c.* 1900).** (*right*)

This cartoon shows Harold Begbie's (1871–1929)
creation Cobbledick of Wam-Wam, an example of
the kind of crude caricature considered acceptable
by publishers at the time but acknowledged
to be highly offensive today. The magazine's
founder, Charles Burgess Fry (1872–1956), was an
international sportsman of renown, who captained
Sussex and England in cricket, gained an England
cap for football and jointly held the world long-jump
record. He was also a philanthropist, a writer, a
diplomat (he served with the Indian delegation at
the League of Nations) and a politician, standing
several times for Parliament. He wrote numerous
books and launched two boys' magazines, *C.B. Fry's
Magazine* and *The Captain*.

JJ Prospectuses of Journals 23 (43b)

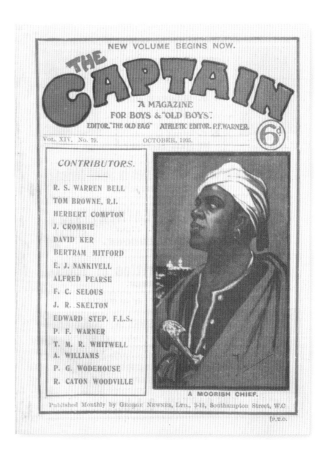

The Captain, a magazine for boys and 'old boys' published between 1899 and 1924. (*above*)

This issue from October 1905 shows 'a Moorish chief'. This was launched by C.B. Fry after *C.B. Fry's Magazine*. It was notable for publishing some of P.G. Wodehouse's early works, including 'Public School Boxing' and the adventures of Psmith. Like other boys' magazines, it often included free gifts and pull-outs, such as a folding plate of South African cricketers.

JJ Prospectuses of Journals 11 (14)

Henry Arthur Jones's play *Carnac Sahib*, produced by Sir Herbert Beerbohm Tree (1853–1917) at Her Majesty's Theatre Haymarket, 10 May 1899. (*right*)

The *New York Times* of 13 April 1899 described the dazzle of Oriental costume, military display and the rattle of drums. Scenes included an English club in the tropics, a palm-shaded river, a jewelled palace, and the 'livid Indian night, the magenta dawn'. It featured 'British officers hemmed in by mutinous and bloodthirsty Rajahs' and displayed 'vividly the warp and woof of Western empire in the East'. The central theme was the struggle of the British Raj to quell mutinous native rajahs. The eponymous hero, played by Tree himself, was Colonel Stacey Carnac.

JJ London Playbills Her Majesty's 2 (2)

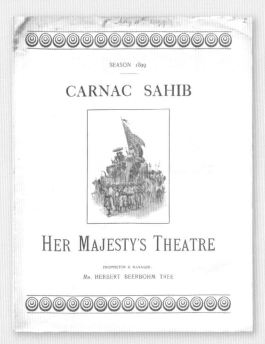

The programme for *Under One Flag*, performed at the Empire Theatre of Varieties, 24 January 1898. (*left*)

This 'imperial ballet' was the Empire Theatre's offering for the 1897 Jubilee year, opening on Jubilee Day, 21 June, and running for a total of thirty-two weeks. Devised and produced by Katti Lanner, it comprised two tableaux. The first featured dancers from England, Ireland, Scotland and Wales outside Windsor Castle. The second, a homage to the Queen–Empress set against a backdrop of a statue of the Queen, involved dancers from all over the Empire. The play ended with a grand cantata involving the whole assembly. It was intended to represent the unity of the United Kingdom in 1837, the start of Victoria's reign and the imperial unity that was a feature of the Empire in the 1890s.

JJ London Playbills Elephant and Castle-Empire (41)

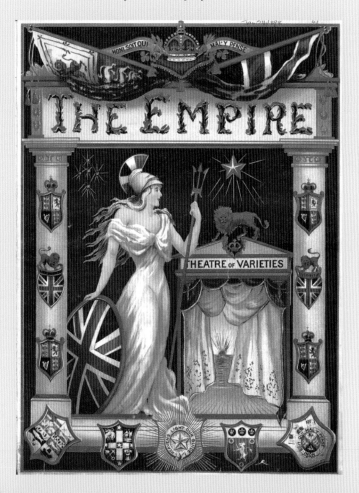

The Imperial Souvenir, a fascinating publication from Christmas 1897. (*right*)

Published by David Nutt of the Strand, the book reproduces a verse from the National Anthem, 'God Save the Queen', in fifty of the languages spoken in the British Empire. The less than inspired verse employed for the purpose was:

> Thy choicest gifts in store
> On her be pleased to pour;
> Long may she reign:
> May she defend our laws,
> And ever give us cause
> To sing with heart and voice,
> God Save the Queen.

Languages included Creole, Gaelic, Greek, Hindi, Hausa and Swahili. Note the detail around the edges of the verses, including buildings typical of the lands from which the languages originate.

JJ Ceremonial Box 3

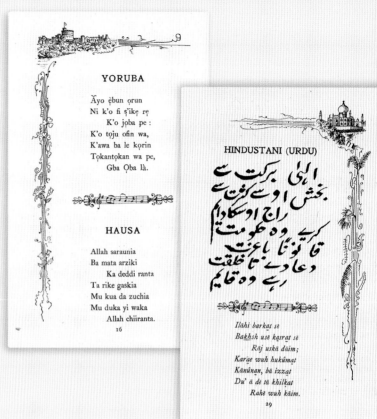

YORUBA

Ãyo ẹbun ọrun
Ni k'o fi şike rẹ
    K'o jọba pe :
K'o tọju ofin wa,
K'awa ba le kọrin
Tọkantọkan wa pe,
    Gba Ọba là.

HAUSA

Allah saraunia
Ba mata arziki
    Ka deddi ranta
Ta rike gaskia
Mu kua da zuchia
Mu duka yi waka
    Allah chiiranta.
16

HINDUSTANI (URDU)

Ilāhi barkat sē
Ba*kh*sh usē kasrat sē
Rāj uskā dāim;
Karāe wuh hukūmat
Kānūnan, bā izzat
Du' ā dē tā *kh*ilkat
Rahē wuh kāim.
29

MUSICAL BOUQUET

JULLIEN'S FAREWELL TO ENGLAND WALTZ.
A COMPANION TO HIS CELEBRATED "PRIMA DONNA WALTZ."

Jullien's 'Farewell to England Waltz', c. early 1840s. (*left*)

Louis Antoine Jullien (1812–1860) was a French composer who made a name conducting promenade concerts in London, though he spent his last years in a French debtors' prison and died in an asylum. The foot of the sheet advertises Henry Russell's (1812–1900) 'Emigrant's Progress Quadrille' and 'The Slave Sale', further indicating the presence of imperial and wider-world themes in popular music.

JJ Emigration Box 1

**A Tour through the British Colonies
and Foreign Possessions, board game
by John Betts from the mid-1850s.**

The game starts and finishes in London (the dome
of St Paul's can be seen in the central illustration),
emphasizing the status of Britain and its capital
city. Players left Britain via Heligoland (a British
territory off the Danish coast in the North Sea,
ceded to Germany in 1890 in return for Germany
acknowledging the paramountcy of British interests
in Zanzibar). They travelled to India via the
Mediterranean and the overland route, or via the
Cape of Good Hope. The game also featured stops at
Niagara Falls in North America, and a jaunt around
the mainland of Australia. Players were permitted
to roll again if they alighted on Jamaica, in order to
mark Britain's role in abolishing the slave trade.

JJ Games Folder (25a)

A TOUR THROUGH THE BRITISH COLONIES, AND FOREIGN POSSESSIONS.

JOHN BETTS, 115 STRAND.

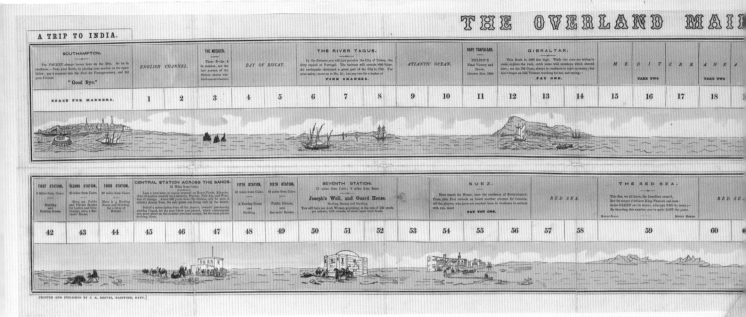

The Overland Mail board game (nineteenth century). (*above*)

The object of the game is to get the Royal Mail delivered around the world.

JJ Games Folder (27)

Lord Dundreary's Voyage to Brother Sam (c. 1833). (*right*)

A globe-trotting board game that takes on the Cape of Good Hope, Australia, Cape Verde Islands, New Zealand, the Sandwich Islands, the North Pole, Iceland and Eskimo territory. Lord Dundreary, a caricature of the brainless aristocrat, was made famous in the play *Our American Cousin* by Tom Taylor (1817–1880). It premiered in 1858; the character, sporting huge sideburns ('dundrearies'), was brought to life on stage by Edward Sothern. Abraham Lincoln was watching a performance of the play in 1865 when he was assassinated.

JJ Games Folder (26)

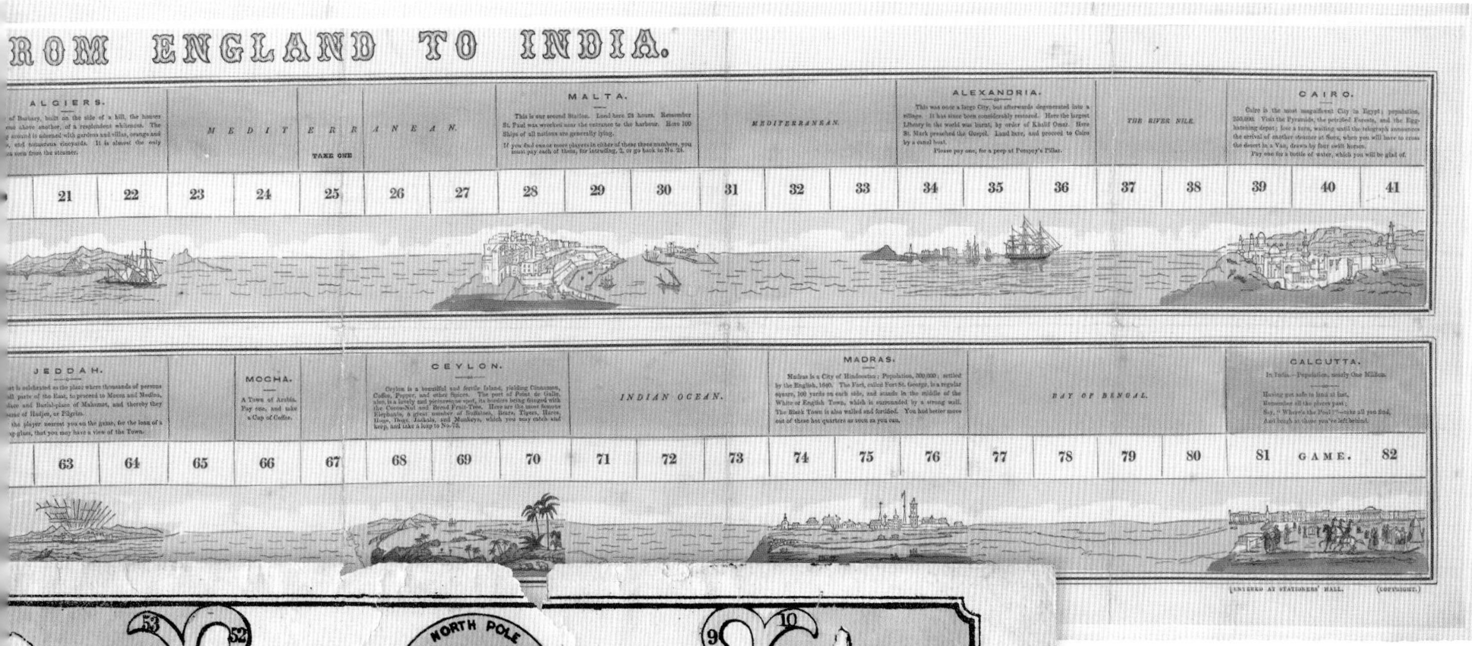

ROM ENGLAND TO INDIA.
ALGIERS.
MEDITERRANEAN.
TAKE ONE
MALTA.
This is our second Station. Land here 24 hours. Remember St. Paul was wrecked near the entrance to the harbour. Here 100 Ships of all nations are generally lying.
If you find one or more players in either of these three numbers, you must pay each of them, for intruding, 2, or go back to No. 24.
MEDITERRANEAN.
ALEXANDRIA.
This was once a large City, but afterwards degenerated into a village. It has since been considerably restored. Here the largest Library in the world was burnt, by order of Khalif Omar. Here St. Mark preached the Gospel. Land here, and proceed to Cairo by a canal boat.
Please pay one, for a peep at Pompey's Pillar.
THE RIVER NILE.
CAIRO.
Cairo is the most magnificent City in Egypt; population, 250,000. Visit the Pyramids, the petrified Forests, and the Egg-hatching depot; lose a turn, waiting until the telegraph announces the arrival of another steamer at Suez, when you will have to cross the desert in a Van, drawn by four swift horses.
Pay one for a bottle of water, which you will be glad of.
21 22 23 24 25 26 27 28 29 30 31 32 33 34 35 36 37 38 39 40 41
JEDDAH.
MOCHA.
A Town of Arabia. Pay one, and take a Cup of Coffee.
CEYLON.
Ceylon is a beautiful and fertile Island, yielding Cinnamon, Coffee, Pepper, and other Spices. The port of Point de Galle, also, is a lovely and picturesque spot, its borders being fringed with the Cocoa-Nut and Bread Fruit-Tree. Here are the most famous Elephants, a great number of Buffaloes, Bears, Tigers, Hares, Hogs, Dogs, Jackals, and Monkeys, which you may catch and keep, and take a leap to No. 73.
INDIAN OCEAN.
MADRAS.
Madras is a City of Hindoostan; Population, 300,000; settled by the English, 1640. The Fort, called Fort St. George, is a regular square, 100 yards on each side, and stands in the middle of the White or English Town, which is surrounded by a strong wall. The Black Town is also walled and fortified. You had better move out of these hot quarters as soon as you can.
BAY OF BENGAL.
CALCUTTA.
In India.—Population, nearly One Million.
Having got safe to land at last,
Remember all the pieces past;
Say, "Where's the Pool?"—take all you find,
And laugh at those you've left behind.
63 64 65 66 67 68 69 70 71 72 73 74 75 76 77 78 79 80 81 GAME. 82
(ENTERED AT STATIONERS' HALL. (COPYRIGHT.)

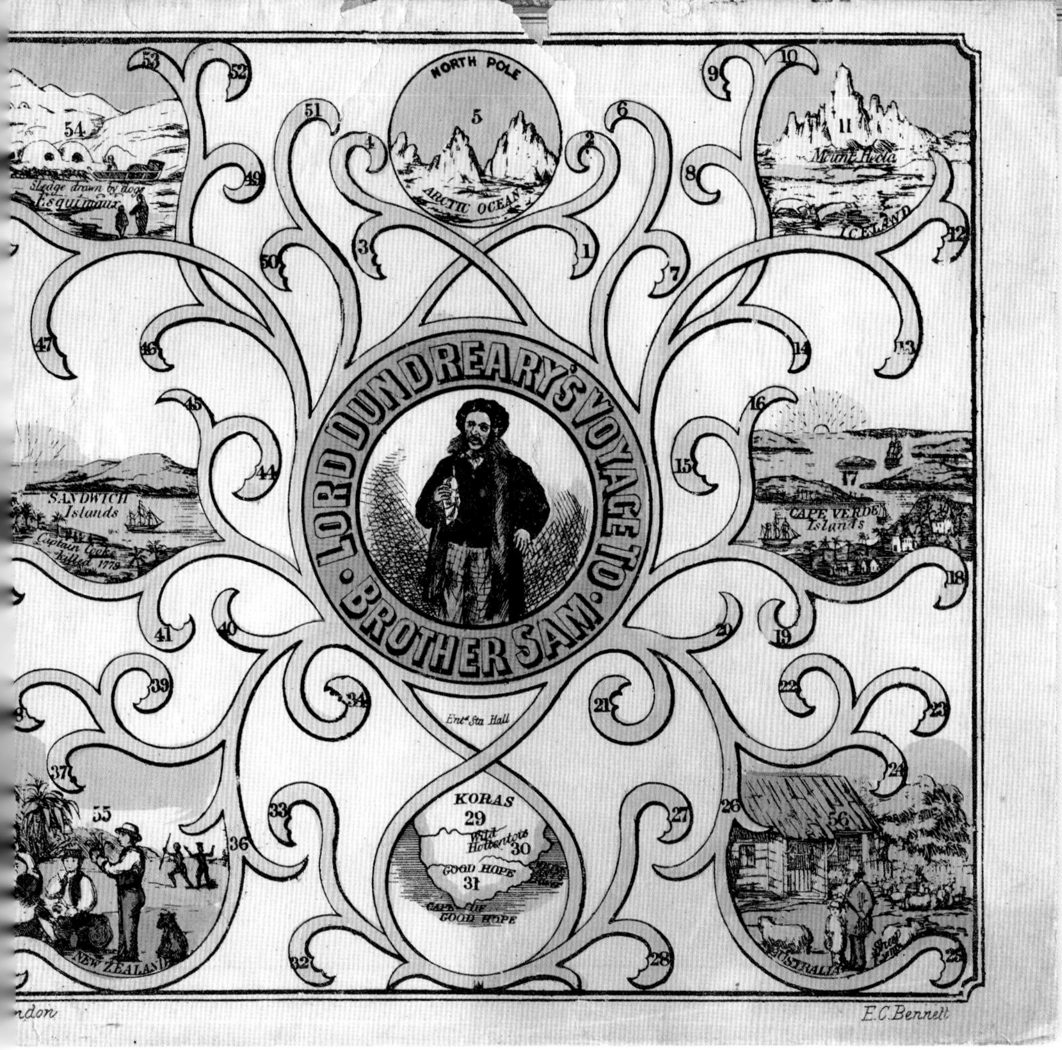

LORD DUNDREARY'S VOYAGE TO BROTHER SAM
NORTH POLE
ARCTIC OCEAN
Mount Hecla
ICELAND
54
Sledge drawn by dogs
Esquimaux
SANDWICH Islands
Captain Cook killed 1779
CAPE VERDE Islands
17
Entd. Sta Hall
KORAS
29
Wild Hottentots
30
GOOD HOPE
31
CAPE OF GOOD HOPE
55
NEW ZEALAND
56
AUSTRALIA
ndon
E.C.Bennett

The Boer War Game (*c.* 1900).

Other contemporary games included The War in South Africa, which had both an adult and a children's version, and Called to Arms: A New Military Game.

JJ Artefacts: Games

LADYSMITH.

MAFEKING.

PRETORIA.

BLOEMFONTEIN.

Pirate and Traveller 1906 board game (California edition).

This game illustrates the manner in which the world was presented as a place of adventure to young children.

JJ Games Folder (32)

THE BOER WAR GAME.
(COPYRIGHT)

1. The Game consists of four sets of counters, the red and white representing the forces of the British, the others those of the Boers; and four cards each representing one of the four towns, viz.:—Pretoria, Ladysmith, Mafeking, and Bloemfontein.

2. Each set contains six small counters and one large counter of the same colour. The large counter is used to press the edge of the smaller ones, thus making them spring or jump forward.

3. The Game can be played by four persons, those holding the red and white counters being in partnership against those using the green and orange, or it can be played by each holding his own individual counters and playing all against all. When two are playing together as partners a player may play with his own or his partner's counters, whichever may be most advantageous to their side.

4. The Game is played on any ordinary table, which should be covered with a table-cloth, a plain green one for preference, on which a large circle should be marked in chalk, the circle representing the battle-field. The circle is not absolutely necessary, except where greater accuracy is required; if no circle is used, the whole of the table-cloth will represent the battle-field.

5. Each player selects which town he is to occupy with his army, and having done so takes his set of counters, placing the small ones in a row on the edge of the circle or table-cloth, retaining the large counter in his hand to play with; and the card bearing the name of his town he places in front of him on the battle-field about six inches from the edge.

6. Each player plays alternately, the object being to kill the men of the opposing armies, and the player whose men are last left on the field is of course the winner.

7. A player kills his opponent by getting his counter on the top of his opponent's counter. The one need not entirely cover the other, but may merely rest upon it. If two or more counters of the same army rest upon each other, and the opponent flips his counter on to the top one, he takes them all, but if his counter only rests upon the lower one only that one is taken. After killing a man, a player is entitled to another turn.

8. The counters must all be fired from the edge of the circle before those on the battle-field may be played with.

9. A counter is considered dead if it goes outside the circle or off the table-cloth and remains there, but if it rolls outside and then back into the circle, it is still alive. A counter is also dead if it falls on to one of the cards belonging to an opponent.

10. The stronger army must always attack the weaker; for instance, if one player has four men alive and another only two, the stronger player must at each shot try to kill one of his opponent's men, whereas the weaker player is not compelled to do so, but may move about the battle-field avoiding his enemy as much as possible.

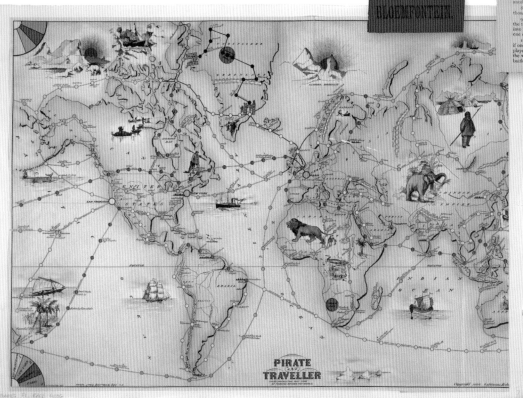

PIRATE
AND
TRAVELLER

Recruiting for Kitchener's Army (*c.* 1915)

A patriotic board game that encouraged
boys to join up for service in the First World
War, and to look after their health (though
for many thousands of young men, being in
Kitchener's Army was a far greater health
risk than smoking). The famous recruiting
poster, 'Your Country Needs You', showing
a moustachioed Lord Kitchener pointing
at the viewer, indicated his status. He was
a soldier–hero who had earned fame in
colonial campaigns in the late nineteenth
and twentieth centuries, notably the Sudan
(hence Kitchener of Khartoum, when he
was ennobled) and South Africa. He was
Commander-in-Chief India (1902–09),
where his power was demonstrated by his
victory over Viceroy Lord Curzon over the
issue of army reform, which led the latter to
resign. He was made Field Marshal in 1909,
and served as Consul General in Egypt. He
was, however, a poor choice as Secretary of
State for War, because none of his civilian
colleagues, with the notable exception
of Winston Churchill, was prepared to
challenge him, contributing to inactivity in
Britain's war leadership and stalemate on the
Western Front. His death in 1916, when he
drowned at sea after HMS *Hampshire* struck
a mine, enabled the British government
to reorganize and move on. The power of
Kitchener and Admiral Lord Fisher at the
Admiralty ensured that, from the First World
War onwards, civilian politicians made
strenuous efforts to subject military leaders to
their ultimate control.

JJ Games Folder (41)

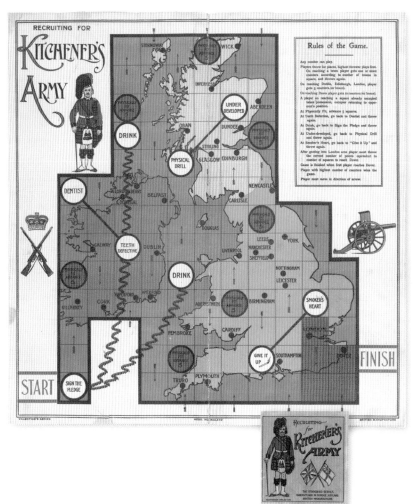

171

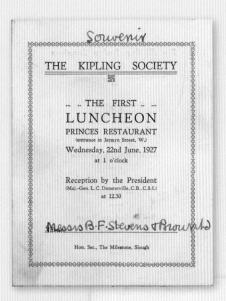

THE KIPLING SOCIETY

卐

... .. THE FIRST .. ...

LUNCHEON
PRINCES RESTAURANT
(entrance in Jermyn Street, W.)
Wednesday, 22nd June, 1927
at 1 o'clock

Reception by the President
(Maj.-Gen. L. C. Dunsterville, C.B., C.S.I.)
at 12.30

Messrs B. F. Stevens & Brown Ltd

Hon. Sec., The Milestone, Slough

Souvenir

The Kipling Society Luncheon

卐

For the bread that you eat and the
biscuits you nibble,
The sweets that you suck and the
joints that you carve,
They are brought to you daily by all
us big steamers,
And if anyone hinders our coming,
you'll starve. "*Big Steamers.*"

It is not wealth, nor talk, nor trade, nor
schools, nor even the Vote
Will save your land, when . . .
hand is tightening ro . . .
But a King and a People . . .
trust each other in all . . .
Can sleep on their bed wit . . .
for the world will leav . . .

C. LUFF & CO., PRINTERS, SLOUGH

The Kipling Society Luncheon
Menu

卐

Hors d'Oeuvres Riche

———

Oeufs Pochés Florentine

———

Saumon Froid, Sauce Verte

———

Poulet Grillé à l'Américaine
Salade de Romaine

———

Soufflé Glacé aux Fraises
Friandises

———

Café

The Kipling Society Luncheon
Programme

卐

12.30   RECEPTION BY THE PRESIDENT AND
        MRS. DUNSTERVILLE
1.0   LUNCHEON
1.30   *Toast*: "THE KING"   THE PRESIDENT
1.35   *Toast*: "RUDYARD KIPLING"
        SIR HARRY BRITTAIN,
           K.B.E., C.M.G., LL.D., M.P.
1.50   A Kipling Song
        JOHN ANDREWS, A.R.C.M.
2.0   *Toast*: "THE KIPLING SOCIETY"
        THE PRESIDENT
2.10   A Kipling Song
        JOHN ANDREWS, A.R.C.M.
2.20   GREETINGS FROM OVERSEA MEMBERS
2.30   "GOD SAVE THE KING"

*(The room is reserved till 4 o'clock if members
desire to stay)*

Menu card and invitation for the Kipling Society's inaugural luncheon held in June 1927.

The Society was founded by J.H.C. Brooking; other founder members included Major General L.C. Dunsterville and G.C. Beresford, the models respectively for Stalky and M'Turk in Kipling's novel *Stalky & Co.* Note the swastika: swastikas appeared on the covers and spines of many of Kipling's books. However, this use had nothing to do with National Socialism, and indeed in 1933 Kipling dropped the swastika out of disgust, having learned of its employment in Germany. The word 'swastika' derives from Sanskrit, and the cross – with either right- or left-leaning branches – had been used by many societies around the world before it was appropriated by the Nazis. It was employed by Buddhists, Jains and Hindus – hence the Anglo-Indian Kipling's adoption of it. For Hindus, it is associated with night-time, magic and the goddess Kali.

JJ Kipling (Rudyard) Box

Title page and pages from
The Absent-Minded Beggar
by Rudyard Kipling (1899).

The Absent-Minded Beggar was a patriotic poem by Kipling highlighting the efforts of the common British soldier in the South African war. It was illustrated by Caton Woodville, and set to music by Sir Arthur Sullivan. It became a national hit, capturing the jingoistic spirit of many British people, and helped raise about a quarter of a million pounds for soldiers' charities.

JJ Kipling (Rudyard) Box

"He's an absent-minded beggar,
But he heard his country call"

WHEN you've shouted 'Rule Britannia,' when you've sung
'God save the Queen,'
When you've finished killing Kruger with your mouth,
Will you kindly drop a shilling in my little tambourine
For a gentleman in *kharki* ordered South?
He's an absent-minded beggar, and his weaknesses are great—
But we and Paul must take him as we find him—
He is out on active service, wiping something off a slate—
And he's left a lot of little things behind him!
Duke's son—cook's son—son of a hundred kings—
(Fifty thousand horse and foot going to Table Bay!)
Each of 'em doing his country's work
(and who's to look after their things?)
Pass the hat for your credit's sake,
and pay—pay—pay!

There are girls he married secret, asking no permission to,
For he knew he wouldn't get it if he did.
There is gas and coals and vittles, and the houserent falling due,
And it's more than rather likely there's a kid.
There are girls he walked with casual. They'll be sorry now
he's gone,
For an absent-minded beggar they will find him,
But it ain't the time for sermons with the winter coming on,
We must help the girl that Tommy's left behind him!
Cook's son—duke's son—son of a belted earl—
Son of a Lambeth publican—it's all the same to-day!
Each of 'em doing his country's work
(and who's to look after the girl?)
Pass the hat for your credit's sake,
and pay—pay—pay!

JUBILEES
AND EXHIBITIONS

A distinctive feature of British culture was the presentation of the Empire and the wider world to the British public in a highly visual form through national events such as Empire Day, coronations and jubilees, and through the extravagant exhibitions that became fashionable in the late nineteenth century. This chapter is essentially a subset of the previous chapter, reviewing images associated with moments of royal ritual and exhibitions such as the Great Exhibition of 1851, the 1924 British Empire Exhibition at Wembley, and the Glasgow Empire Exhibition of 1938. In addition to these set-piece exhibitions, there were more focused exhibitions such as 'Jamaica in London' and the 'Stanley and Africa' exhibition. Such events sought to showcase the Empire, its produce and variety, but were also strident propaganda for the justness of British rule, often confirming common racial stereotypes. They functioned as propaganda, business, education and entertainment combined.

A wide range of overseas countries and their people were featured in ambitious exhibitions in British cities. Both Venice and the Niagara Falls were re-created in London; 'the Levant' and 'the Orient' had their own exhibitions in the capital; and events boasting Indian or colonial pavilions and 'genuine' Zulu villages were common. These events portrayed British rule as uncontroversial and part of the established order of things.[1] The exhibition vogue really began with the Great Exhibition of 1851, and at the 1862 London Exhibition the Empire was well represented, including 7,000 items from India and material from thirty other colonies. The 1886 Colonial and Indian Exhibition was a conscious attempt to demonstrate the wealth and industrial development of the Empire, planned by a Royal Commission and opened by the Queen in a ceremony at which the National Anthem was sung in Sanskrit and an ode by Tennyson was set to music by Sir Arthur Sullivan of Gilbert and Sullivan fame. The Crystal Palace Empire exhibition of 1911 'was intended to demonstrate to the somewhat casual, often times unobservant British public the real significance of our great self-governing Dominions, to make us familiar with their products, their ever-increasing resources, their illimitable possibilities'.[2]

The imperial exhibitions of 1911, 1924 and 1938 were major events that sought to bring the Empire and the world to the British public. The Wembley Empire Exhibition occupied 216 acres of farmland and featured fifteen miles of walkways connecting the pavilions of nearly eighty of the Empire's colonies and dominions. 'There were Burmese dancers, Malayan basket-makers, Ashanti weavers, and Nigerian rice-pounders.'[3] The Exhibition was a recognition of the imperial contribution during the First World War (the Prince of Wales, a couple of years before, had embarked on a major Empire Tour for this purpose as well) and was also designed as an advertisement for imperial trade and migration.

Military tattoos were a feature of British life just like the Epsom Derby or the Oxford and Cambridge Boat Race. The Royal Tournament, the Aldershot Military Tattoo, and numerous ad hoc events such as Imre Kiralfy's celebration of the relief of the European legations in China during the Boxer Rebellion, presented imperial themes to the public. Tattoos allowed British royal and military pageantry to come together for the delectation of the public, massaging national pride and contributing to British prestige in the wider world. This was show-business empire, intended to thrill, inform and make money. These military festivals often made specific reference to empire, as at the 1936 Aldershot Tattoo when the attack on Rangoon over a century before was re-enacted. Such displays asserted the potency of the British Army and the continuing mission of the Royal Navy to defend the sea lanes of the world. In the 1920s, the Hendon Air Pageant re-enacted events such as the bombardment of native villages, demonstrating the junior service's role in imperial policing.

Empire on show took other forms, too. Waxwork displays reproduced famous imperial figures, and city halls held exhibitions of art or photographs chronicling the overseas ventures of explorers and maritime expeditions. *Success* was a former convict ship that showed what life was like at sea for the hapless individuals banished to the Australian colonies, the victims of the early decades of the nineteenth century becoming the entertainment of the latter.

Programme for the Adelaide Jubilee International Exhibition of 1887.

The jubilee was that of Queen Victoria, commemorating her fiftieth year on the throne. The city of Adelaide was named after William IV's consort. The illustration encapsulates a range of familiar colonial narratives: the benefits of empire are shown through international trade (goods shipped to Australia from Calcutta, Canada and Britain), loyalty to the Queen, progress signalled by the background train, and friendship and a maternal relationship with the indigenous inhabitants.

JJ Exhibition Catalogues Box 24

The diamond jubilee of Canadian confederation, 1867–1927.

The cover of this souvenir brochure shows the British coat of arms and stereotypical depictions of Canada's various peoples.

JJ Empire & Colonies Box 3

Commemorative souvenir brochures (1938–46).

Celebrating proud new countries and provinces, these publications marked the 150th anniversary of the first British settlement of Australia (1938) and the 60th anniversary of the naming and incorporation of Vancouver (1946). Vancouver adopted its new name in 1886, when the town was incorporated. Prior to this, the settlement had been known as Granville, and before that, from the first permanent white settlement in 1865, as Gastown. The area was originally home to the Salish tribe and had been visited by the Spanish explorer José Maria Narvaez in 1791. Vancouver Island was sighted by Captain Cook in 1778; four years later the site of what was to become the settlement of Vancouver was visited by the British naval officer Captain George Vancouver. Embarked on a global surveying mission, by the time he returned to Britain in 1795 his ship had circumnavigated the world, travelling 65,000 miles and charting over 10,000 miles of new coast. Vancouver developed as a hub of the timber trade, known for its wood processing and rail and sea links, and came to surpass the nearby city of Victoria in this role.

JJ Empire & Colonies Box 3

Postcards from the 1911 Festival of Empire Exhibition.

The exhibition was held in and around the Crystal Palace, the structure originally built in Hyde Park for the 1851 Great Exhibition and relocated to Sydenham Hill in 1854, where it stood until destroyed by fire in 1936. The 1911 exhibition opened on 12 May and was held to commemorate the coronation of King George V. It featured three-quarter-sized models of the Empire's parliamentary buildings and a pageant of the history of London, England and the Empire. There was also a major inter-imperial sports championship, forerunner of the Empire (later Commonwealth) Games.

JJ Postcards

British Empire Exhibition (1924).

Striking postcards showing the Indian Courtyard
and the Australia Pavilion. Note the stylish British
lion, the Exhibition's logo.

JJ Postcards

**British Empire
Exhibition (1924).**

The guide for the Palestine
pavilion.

JJ Exhibition Catalogues Box 24

Visually appealing literature from the 1938 British Empire Exhibition in Glasgow's Bellahouston Park.

Glasgow was a major imperial city, often referred to as the Empire's workshop or the 'second city of the Empire'. The Exhibition, with its stunning modern buildings, water features and Tower of Empire, was visited by over 13 million people during the six months it was open. During the Exhibition the Cunard liner *Queen Elizabeth* was launched from the city.

JJ Exhibition Catalogues Box 20

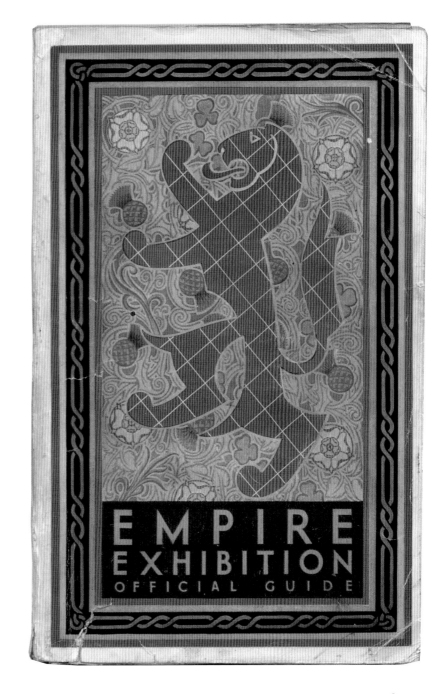

Empire of India Exhibition, Earl's Court, 1895.

The message of this Imre Kiralfy extravaganza was that enlightened British rule had created modern India. Paintings and moving pictures underlined the classic Victorian message and its vision of India. As well as these didactic messages about the goodness of British rule, entertainment was always a key feature of imperial exhibitions. For many people the entertainment – 'nice day out' – aspect outweighed the educative intentions of organizers. As Noël Coward said about the 1924 British Empire Exhibition at Wembley, 'I've brought you here to see the wonders of the Empire and all you want to do is go on the dodgems.' And when P.G. Wodehouse's Bertie Wooster was dragged to the Exhibition, he sloped off as soon as he could and made for the Planters' Bar. At the Empire of India Exhibition, there was a 300-foot Ferris wheel, offering splendid views of London.

JJ Exhibition Catalogues Box 24

The dramatic cover of the 1894 programme for 'The Orient at Olympia'.

This was one of the many shows put on by Imre Kiralfy (1845–1919), who was born into a Hungarian family of dancers, musicians and acrobats. He achieved fame in Britain and America as the organizer of dance-based spectaculars in city centres. He organized the Venice in London show (1891) and the Empire of India Exhibition (1895). When he had outgrown Earl's Court, he built the great White City at Shepherd's Bush, scene of the 1908 Olympic Games. He died in Brighton and left an estate worth £136,000. His brother, Bolossy Kiralfy (1847–1932), was also involved in the business, and this Olympia show included performances of *The Orient* by the Italian-born composer Paola Giorza (1832–1914). Giorza had worked in Australia for much of the 1870s and in 1884 published his dance music book *Souvenir d'Australia*. Imre Kiralfy was a British citizen and clearly something of an imperial patriot. He was a Freemason and a member of the British Empire League, formed in 1895 to promote imperialism and imperial unity.

JJ Exhibition Catalogues Box 24

Palestine in London (1907). (*left*)

Not all imperial or 'wider world' exhibitions were about entertainment and show; some had the pursuit of knowledge as their main preoccupation. In the summer of 1907 Reverend Samuel Schor organized a 'gigantic' Palestine Exhibition that strove to 'combine all that is interesting, fascinating, and instructive about the East'. The Exhibition also covered Ancient Egypt, Assyria and Babylon, and its twelve divisions included 'agriculture' (featuring a working farm), 'industry and art' (featuring a carpenter's shop in Nazareth) and a section revealing 'how Easterners live' (featuring a Bedouin encampment). Ten years later, General Allenby conquered Jerusalem, and Palestine became part of the British Empire.

JJ Exhibition Catalogues Box 24

Niagara in London (1890). (*right*)

'Nature's grandest wonder exhibited in the world's greatest city.'

JJ Exhibition Catalogues Box 24

Programme for the Greater Britain exhibition held at Earl's Court in 1899.

The exhibition featured motion pictures sponsored by the Queensland government, a mining section connected with Cecil Rhodes, and a show featuring 200 Zulu warriors, typical of the zoo-like aspect of this type of event. During the exhibition the Empress Theatre had twice-daily showings of 'Savage South Africa', and the Australian theatre Elysia showed 'Jesse Jewell's Australian Marionettes'.

JJ Exhibition Catalogues Box 20

The Stanley and African exhibition at the Victoria Gallery in London in 1890. (*below*)

This exhibition was more about education than spectacle. What passed as scholarship underpinned a range of contemporary clichés about Africa viewed through Western eyes. Science, art, anthropology and entertainment combined in the exhibition, which consciously sought to develop the celebrity status of Henry Morton Stanley.

JJ Exhibition Catalogues Box 24

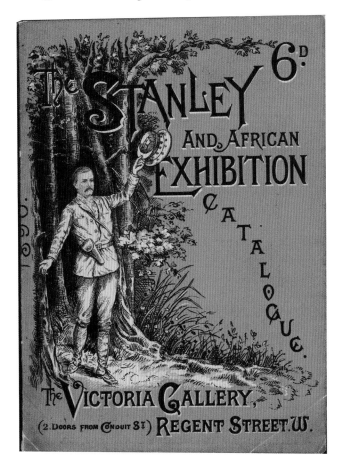

Royal Military Tournament, Agricultural Hall, 1905, celebrating the centenary of the Battle of Trafalgar.

JJ Military & Naval Pageants Box

Programme for a 'military spectacle' organized by Imre Kiralfy at Earl's Court in 1900.

The show was called 'China, or the Relief of the Legations', and demonstrated the manner in which notable overseas events were speedily represented in popular culture back at home, usually in an uncompromisingly patriotic light. The Boxer Rebellion was a complex movement stimulated by anti-foreign sentiment induced by imperial expansion, such as the activities of Christian missionaries, and public dissatisfaction regarding the incapacity and corruption of the Chinese state. In June 1900 Boxer forces besieged the embassies of the foreign powers in Peking, and persuaded the Empress Dowager to declare war on the foreigners. An eight-nation alliance was formed in response, led by Britain, which contributed over 12,000 marines and soldiers, together with considerable naval forces, to the subsequent campaign to relieve the legations. The resulting defeat of the Boxers led the external powers to impose humiliating terms upon the Chinese government, contributing to its growing weakness and unpopularity, and ultimately leading to the 1911 revolution and the demise of the Qing dynasty.

JJ Military & Naval Pageants Box

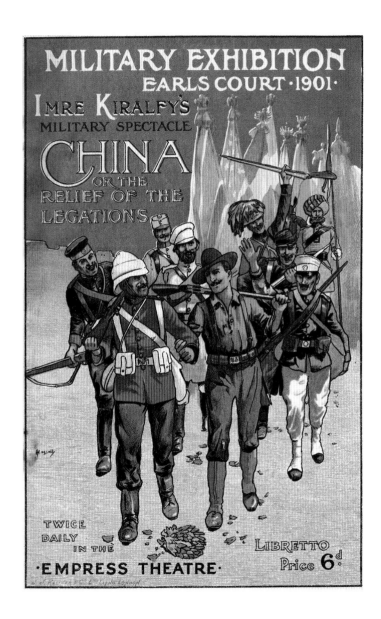

The British Army policing the Empire's borders: the attack on the stockades at Rangoon, 1824. (*below*)

This was a military re-enactment for the 1936 Aldershot Tattoo, a classic rendition of an episode from Britain's colonial past, played out for the sake of entertainment and in order to celebrate Britain's military prowess and heritage. The attack took place during the first of Britain's three nineteenth-century wars with the kingdom of Burma, which eventually saw the entire country annexed when Lord Randolph Churchill was Secretary of State for India in 1886.

JJ Military & Naval Pageants Box

Programme for the Aldershot Military Tattoo of June 1936.
(*above*)

The illustration shows a typical representation of chivalry coupled with martial themes.

JJ Military & Naval Pageants Box

The programme for the Royal Tournament held at Olympia in spring 1939. (*right*)

This was the last big military pageant before the outbreak of the Second World War, and the picture reflects both the imminence of war and the drive for rearmament in the 1930s. The guardsman represents tradition and timelessness, but the bombers illustrate the great significance of air power and the threat of large-scale bombing; the prime minister, Stanley Baldwin, had predicted that 'the bomber would always get through'. Thus as the Second World War approached, strategy and doctrine took it as given that German bombers would cause thousands of casualties in British cities from the moment they took to the skies, and that Britain's only way of hurting the enemy was to try to do exactly the same to them.

JJ Military & Naval Pageants Box

'Visit Jamaica in the heart of London'.

Through the efforts of the Jamaica Chamber of Commerce, the island was first represented at the British Industries Fair in 1935, held at London's Olympia Exhibition Hall.

JJ Exhibition Catalogues Box 24

EMPIRE AND POLITICS

The ephemera considered in this final chapter demonstrate the manner in which empire contributed to British political life. Empire had wide resonance in British politics. For example, 'empire-focused activism was a central component of middle- and upper-class white women's public work and political engagements' from the eighteenth to the twentieth century.[1] Some imperial issues were central to British politics, sometimes for decades at a time. Slavery, Irish Home Rule, free trade and imperial protection were all topics of political debate, and could determine when elections were called and which political party won them. Joseph Chamberlain, the most egregious imperial politician at the turn of the nineteenth century, 'destroyed the Liberal Party over [Irish] Home Rule, [and] was to destroy the Tory Party on the tariff issue [arguing that non-imperial imports should be taxed]'.[2] The Westminster political structure meant that Irish MPs could make or break governments if neither of the main parties held a clear majority of seats in the House of Commons. In the early years of the twentieth century some of the country's most influential politicians from both major political parties met on the common ground of 'Liberal Imperialism', a political creed which espoused social welfare improvements at home and strong and enlightened imperial policies overseas.

Overseas settlement was at times a topic of heated political debate, creating distinct forms of ephemera as political campaigns were supported by pamphleteers and satirical cartoons. This was the case when the alleged 'horrors' of colonial life were put before the public by the political and moral opponents of emigration, or when the supposedly debilitating demographic effects of emigration on British society were highlighted during campaigns to halt the outflow of migrants. The issue remained controversial and politically charged, and in the 1920s the British government felt the need to rebrand 'emigration'. Leopold Amery, the first Secretary of State for the Dominions, recorded that on assuming office in 1925 'almost my first task was to get rid of the word "emigration", its association of unemployment and expatriation, and to substitute ... "Oversea Settlement" as the object of our policy'.[3]

Events that took place in the colonies (as opposed to matters of imperial policy) could obtrude into British political life in intense fashion. The Indian Mutiny, the Jamaica Rebellion and General Gordon's death in Khartoum were nineteenth-century examples. In the twentieth century the Conservative government's prosecution of the Boer War (1899–1902) was heavily politicized and became a major element in the Liberal Party's landslide election victory in 1906. Earlier in the war, the conquest of the Boer capitals of Johannesburg and Bloemfontein had led to the production of patriotic posters depicting a British-conquered South Africa laid before Queen Victoria and Colonial Secretary Joseph Chamberlain. During the same period, the issue of Chinese 'coolie' labour in the South African mines haunted governments of both parties, and publications such as the *Empire Review* supported Chamberlain's movement for closer

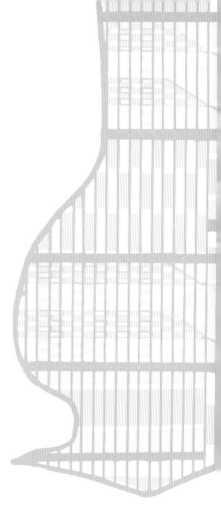

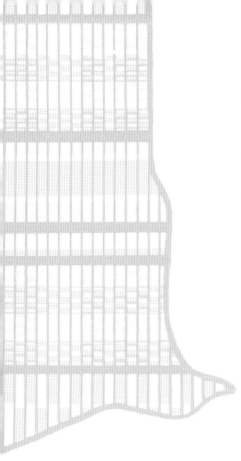

imperial union. The Amritsar Massacre – and conflicting views concerning the actions of Michael O'Dwyer, Governor of the Punjab, and General Reginald Dyer, commander of the troops – led to intense political debate and public meetings. In the 1930s the campaign against the national government's proposed Government of India Bill, led by Winston Churchill, was a prolonged and nationwide political saga. During the decolonization years imperial issues could rear their head on the national political stage, nowhere better demonstrated than during the Suez Crisis of 1956, which led to resignations from the cabinet and the retirement of the prime minister. Later still, Enoch Powell's 'Rivers of Blood' speech, warning of the danger of 'New Commonwealth' immigration into Britain, led to marches and riots on British streets, touching a national nerve that remains sensitive to this day.

Issues of imperial policy and conditions in the colonies fuelled political debate; pamphlets, posters and public meetings were employed to support political campaigns. There were always political movements that were 'for' or 'against' certain imperial policies. Political media often expressed metropolitan outrage at colonial excesses and inveighed against the perceived evils of opium and slavery, or the deleterious effects of emigration. Militarism, imperialism and taxation were highlighted as connected dangers, the 'intolerable suffering of Indians' was deplored, and characters like Cecil Rhodes attracted a great deal of controversy. Another important political theme that left its mark on politics was decolonization. The 1950s and 1960s saw a revolution in global sovereignty as dozens of new nation-states came into existence. New states produced their own iconography as they marked new-found nationhood with flags, anthems and national symbols. In the terminal years of the British Empire the public became familiar with images of liberation struggles, from the Rhodesian Bush War and wars against so-called Communists in Southeast Asia, to the anti-apartheid movement. Meanwhile the images profiled in this volume that had illustrated empire became much more controversial. What had passed as entertainment or advertisement in one age was unacceptable and even offensive in another.

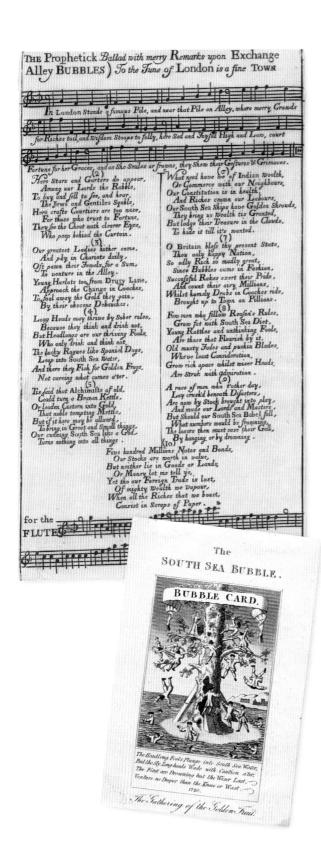

**Assorted ephemera relating to the
South Sea Bubble (early eighteenth century).**

The South Sea Bubble was a plan devised by the Lord Treasurer, Robert Harley, for the retirement of the floating national debt. Under the plan the debt, accrued in the War of the Spanish Succession, was assumed by merchants, to whom the government guaranteed annual payments equal to £2 million for a certain period. This sum, amounting to 6 per cent interest, was to be obtained from duties on imports. A monopoly of British trade in the South Seas and South America was given to these merchants, incorporated as the South Sea Company in 1711, and extravagant notions of the riches of South America were fostered ('South Seas' referred to South America and its waters). In the spring of 1720 the company offered to assume practically the whole national debt, at that time equal to more than £80 million. Companies of all kinds were floated to take advantage of the public interest in obtaining South Sea Company stock – one company famously promising to do something profitable 'but no one to know what it is'. The company's staple trade was in slaves, taken to the Americas from West Africa. Speculation soon carried stock to ten times its nominal value. The chairman and some directors sold out, the bubble burst and the stock collapsed. Thousands of stockholders were ruined and suicide was not uncommon. Parliamentary investigation revealed complicity by company officials, and two members of the court of George I were also implicated in the scandal. A political crisis was averted, however, through the efforts of Sir Robert Walpole, the Chancellor of the Exchequer. About one-third of the original capital was recovered for stockholders. Given the magnitude of the crisis, it naturally left its mark on British popular culture. The bubble playing cards appeared in the 1720s, along with cartoons and ditties.

JJ South Sea Company Box 1

India! Opium! & China!

A

PUBLIC CONVERSATION

WILL BE CONDUCTED

ON WEDNESDAY EVENING, FEB. 10th.,

AT THE

CONGREGATIONAL SCHOOL ROOM,

CALEDONIAN ROAD,

BETWEEN

THE REV. E. DAVIES, AND MR. REYNOLDS,

IN WHICH

STARTLING REVELATIONS

Of the demoralizing and destructive effects of Opium on the population of India; its physical, social, and religious effects on the population of China; and the duty of British Christians of both sexes at the present crisis, will be submitted.

The Chair will be taken at Eight o'clock.—FREE ADMISSION.

Warren Hall & Co., Steam Printers and Stationers, 10 Cambridge Terrace, Camden Town. N.W.

A splendid political poster dating from the 1899–1902 Anglo-Boer War. (*below*)

The 'All Red Now Joey' refers to Joseph Chamberlain, the monocled figure depicted. He was the imperialist Colonial Secretary who had overseen British policy in Southern Africa leading up to the war. On the left-hand side is Colonel Robert Baden-Powell, whose defence of the besieged town of Mafeking achieved international fame. The map is dominated by an image of Lord Roberts, the British commander-in-chief.

JJ Empire & Colonies Folder

India! Opium! & China! (mid-nineteenth century). (*above*)

Illustrating the protrusion of imperial issues into British political debate, this poster advertises a public meeting at which 'startling revelations' about the opium trade and the effects of the narcotic were to be made. The venue for the meeting was a Congregational hall and one of the speakers, Reverend E. Davies, was a member of the London Missionary Society. Missionaries played an important role in alerting the public to inequities in the colonies.

JJ Empire & Colonies Folder

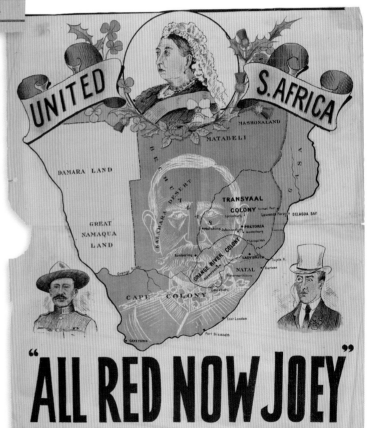

**Pamphlet reproducing a speech
by John Morley (1838–1923).**

Morley was a noted Liberal MP, a former editor of
the *Fortnightly Review* and the *Pall Mall Gazette*,
and a biographer of both Cromwell and Gladstone.
In 1886 Gladstone made Morley chief secretary in
Ireland. The pamphlet illustrates the manner in
which imperial policy could intersect with domestic
politics. A prominent advocate of Home Rule when
he first entered politics, at the time of the Boer War
Morley was known for his anti-imperial views, in
1899 decrying the war in South Africa as unjustified
British expansionism and criticizing the role of
chartered companies and the private interests of
individuals such as Cecil Rhodes. He feared that
interventionist foreign policy and imperialism
would increase the role of the state in society and
unfairly increase the tax burden borne by certain
sectors of the population. The large increase in
state expenditure required to fund the Boer War, he
believed, would lead to government gaining greater
power to interfere in Britain's social and economic
structures. In the 1902 New Year's Honours, Morley
was named as one of the founder members of the new
Order of Merit, and in the 1905 Liberal government
he was made Secretary of State for India. Whilst
in this office he was most notably associated with
the political changes known as the Morley–Minto
reforms (Lord Minto was the Viceroy) which allowed
Indians some formal role in politics (1909). He was
created Viscount Morley of Blackburn in 1908.

JJ Empire & Colonies Box 1

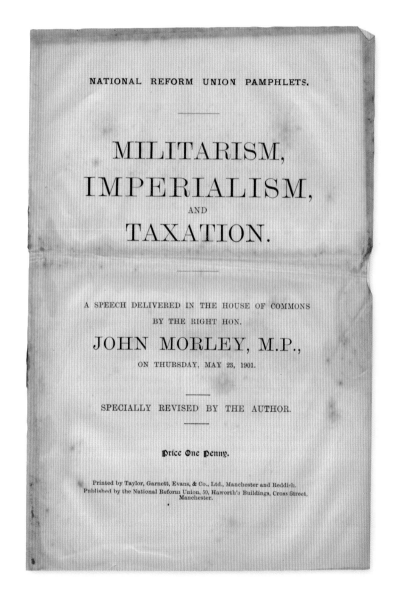

NATIONAL REFORM UNION PAMPHLETS.

MILITARISM, IMPERIALISM, AND TAXATION.

A SPEECH DELIVERED IN THE HOUSE OF COMMONS
BY THE RIGHT HON.

JOHN MORLEY, M.P.,

ON THURSDAY, MAY 23, 1901.

SPECIALLY REVISED BY THE AUTHOR.

Price One Penny.

Printed by Taylor, Garnett, Evans, & Co., Ltd., Manchester and Reddish.
Published by the National Reform Union, 50, Haworth's Buildings, Cross Street,
Manchester.

THIRD YEAR OF PUBLICATION

"THE EMPIRE REVIEW improves in vigour and interest as it matures. It is a great merit in a magazine and its editor to have earned the right to claim that the fourth volume is better than the first, and this right has been fairly won in the case of THE EMPIRE REVIEW and Mr. Kinloch Cooke."
The Overland Mail, *December 1901.*

ONE SHILLING NET   PUBLISHED MONTHLY

WORLD-WIDE CIRCULATION

THE EMPIRE REVIEW

EDITED BY C. KINLOCH COOKE, B.A., LL.M.

St. John's College, Cambridge; Barrister-at-Law

(late Editor of "The Observer," "The Pall Mall Gazette," and "The English Illustrated Magazine");

WE cannot all, following the example of Mr. Chamberlain, go out and study on the spot the various phases of over-sea life. Nor can our kinsmen dwelling in other climes, except in comparatively few instances, journey to the Motherland to inquire into the social and political problems which, in one form or another, find their counterpart in the daily life of the Indian, the Canadian, the Australian, the New Zealander, and the South African.

But EVERYONE can read for themselves

THE STORY OF THE KING'S DOMINIONS
THEIR PEOPLE, THEIR POLICY, AND THEIR TRADE

as told in THE EMPIRE REVIEW, a human document full of vitality and actuality, written by men and women of authority, and breathing sentiments of loyalty to the Throne and devotion to Flag and Country.

The *Empire Review*, edited by C. Kinloch Cooke (1854–1944), of December 1902.
(*above*)

This journal supported imperial protection and the ideas of Joseph Chamberlain for an imperial federation.

JJ Prospectuses of Journals 20 (3)

An anti-Cecil Rhodes publication from the radical *Morning Leader*, c. 1900.
(*below*)

Another example of political pamphleteering, this publication claimed that Rhodes was an 'expensive luxury' that Britain could ill afford.

JJ Empire & Colonies Box 4

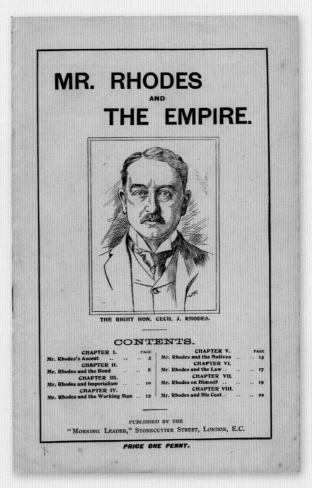

MR. RHODES
AND
THE EMPIRE.

THE RIGHT HON. CECIL J. RHODES.

CONTENTS.

CHAPTER I.	PAGE	CHAPTER V.	PAGE
Mr. Rhodes's Ascent ...	3	Mr. Rhodes and the Natives ...	13
CHAPTER II.		CHAPTER VI.	
Mr. Rhodes and the Bond ...	8	Mr. Rhodes and the Law ...	17
CHAPTER III.		CHAPTER VII.	
Mr. Rhodes and Imperialism ...	10	Mr. Rhodes on Himself ...	19
CHAPTER IV.		CHAPTER VIII.	
Mr. Rhodes and the Working Man	12	Mr. Rhodes and His Cost.. ...	22

PUBLISHED BY THE
"MORNING LEADER," STONECUTTER STREET, LONDON, E.C.

PRICE ONE PENNY.

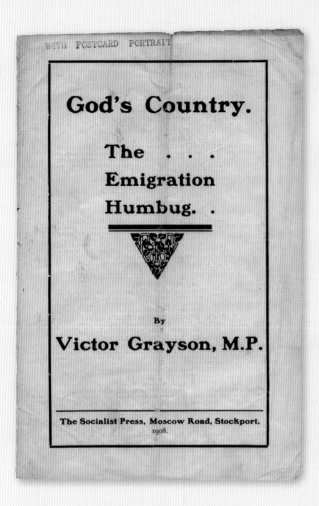

Stricken India, published by the Reform Press. (*below*)

This pamphlet about the horrors of the 1900 Indian famine was issued in an attempt to raise money in Britain for famine relief.

JJ Empire & Colonies Box 2

'The Emigration Humbug'. (*above*)

A pamphlet by Victor Grayson (1908). Grayson was a Member of Parliament opposed to overseas settlement and the evils of slums and cheap labour in Canada. It was published by the Socialist Press, and illustrates the manner in which colonial issues could become a part of political debate within Britain.

JJ Emigration Box 2

IMPEACH THEM!

Are those really responsible for Atrocities in India to go Scot Free?

PUBLIC MEETING

To demand the Recall of Lord Chelmsford

and the Impeachment of Sir M. O'Dwyer,

KINGSWAY HALL,

To=morrow, Thursday, at 7.30.

SPEAKERS:

The Hon. V. J. PATEL
(General Secretary of the Indian National Congress)

GEORGE LANSBURY.

NEIL MACLEAN, M.P.

Major BARNES, M.P.

HELENA NORMANTON, B.A.

H. B. LEES-SMITH (Ex-M.P., Northampton)

B. G. HORNIMAN
and others.

COME AND HELP TO VINDICATE BRITISH HUMANITY!
LANTERN SLIDES OF THE MARTIAL LAW ATROCITIES.

Organ Recital 7 to 7.30.

Kent & Matthews, Ltd., Wandsworth Road, S.W. —31821

Impeach them! (1919).

Indicating the depths of public feeling stirred by the Amritsar massacre, this fly poster advertises a meeting at Kingsway Hall against British policy, illustrated by a magic lantern show of atrocities under martial law, and addressed by MPs including George Lansbury, later leader of the Labour Party, and the general secretary of the Indian National Congress, V.J. Patel. It called for the impeachment of the Governor of the Punjab, Sir Michael O'Dwyer, and the recall of the Viceroy, Lord Chelmsford, who did indeed return to Britain under a cloud soon afterwards.

JJ Empire & Colonies Box 2

The Merdeka Book: Malaya's
Road to Nationhood **(1957).**

This handbook was published by the *Straits Times*
to commemorate the birth of Malaysia on 31 August
1957. *Merdeka* is a Malay word for freedom. As
nationalist movements and decolonization broke
up the British Empire, new words encapsulating
the struggle for freedom, independence or union
with other nations became familiar, such as *enosis*,
swadeshi, *swaraj*, *uhuru* and *merdeka*. Malaya had
by the 1950s become the most valuable part of the
British Empire, and there were plans to make it into
a dominion of Southeast Asia. But the price to pay
for defeating the communist insurgency was the
granting of independence earlier than anticipated.

JJ Empire & Colonies Box 5

Ghana Independence Celebrations (March 1957),

New national symbols were devised by new national governments, attempting to build national identities in erstwhile colonies. A good example of contemporary design as independence came to replace colonial rule, the first image is the official programme for the Independence Celebrations that marked the transformation of the colony of the Gold Coast into the independent nation-state of Ghana, as Governor Sir Charles Arden Clarke handed over to President Kwame Nkrumah. It was a landmark event: Ghana was the first sub-Saharan African colony to gain independence (the Sudan, which gained independence in 1956, had never been a colony; though effectively ruled by the British, it was officially an Anglo-Egyptian condominium, administered through the Foreign Office). The British Parliament passed the Ghana Independence Act in January 1957, and on 6 March the new National Assembly issued a proclamation of independence. Two days later, Ghana joined the United Nations. Decolonization rapidly increased the number of sovereign states in the world and transformed the international landscape. The colours of the new national flag are stylishly displayed within a design based upon the country's borders.

The event was attended by the Duchess of Kent on 4 March 1957 and held at the national stadium in the capital, Accra. The Queen's message, read by the Duchess, declared that 'the hopes of many, especially in Africa, rest on your endeavours'. The ceremony was also attended by Martin Luther King and his wife. There was a fly-past and military display from the departing British; Nkrumah addressed the new nation colourfully dressed in traditional African costume; the new anthem, 'God Bless Our Homeland Ghana' was sung; and the Independence Arch was opened, bearing the national motto 'Freedom and Justice'. The country's coat of arms, granted by the Queen, featured a St George's Cross and the golden lion of the United Kingdom symbolizing close relations between Ghana, Britain and the Commonwealth. It also displayed swords representing regional governments, a castle representing the presidential palace and national government, a cocoa tree representing agriculture, and a gold mine. The star represented the freedom of Africa.

JJ Empire & Colonies Box 4

Ghana Independence Celebrations

Ceremony of National Welcome

to

Her Royal Highness
The Duchess of Kent
C.I., G.C.V.O., G.B.E.

in the

Accra Stadium

at 4 p.m. on Monday 4th March 1957

GHANA
INDEPENDENCE CELEBRATIONS
MARCH 1957   OFFICIAL PROGRAMME   PRICE 6D.

OUR COAT OF ARMS
ITS SIGNIFICANCE

The design of Guyana's Coat of Arms is interpreted as follows :—

The Amerindian head-dress symbolises the Amerindians as the indigenous people of the country. The two diamonds at the side of the head-dress represent the country's mining industry. The helmet is the monarchial insignia. The two jaguars holding a pick-axe, a sugar cane and a stalk of rice symbolise labour and the two main agricultural industries of the country — sugar and rice. The shield which is decorated with the national flower, the Victoria Regia Lily, is to protect the nation. The three blue wavy lines represent the many waters of Guyana. The Canje Pheasant at the bottom of the shield represents a rare bird found principally in this part of the world.

The Coat of Arms was selected on the recommendation of the National History and Arts Council and approved by the College of Arms, England. It was accepted by the House of Assembly on Friday. 25th February, 1966.

THE HERALDIC TERMS

Argent	—	Metal Silver or White
Azure	—	blue
Gules	—	red
Or	—	gold
Vert	—	green
Base	—	lower part
Chief	—	upper part
Dexter	—	right
Sinister	—	left
Fimbriated	—	bordered
Pile	—	a wedge-shaped mass
Fess	—	Horizontal band one third the depth of the shield
Barrulets	—	a diminutive of the bar
Proper	—	represented in its natural colour.

Pamphlet heralding the independence of Guyana (formerly British Guiana) on 26 May 1966.

The British Guiana Independence Conference had convened in London in 1965 and decided upon a new constitution. As in the case of Ghana, the paraphernalia of new-found nationhood combined the new and the traditional with a rather curious backward glance towards dependence upon Britain. The British College of Arms designed the new national emblem; Guyana's new House of Assembly then adopted it.

JJ Empire & Colonies Box 4

Guyana

SYMBOLS OF NATIONHOOD

MAY
1966

AFTERWORD

There was always a blurred line between things 'imperial' and things simply to do with the non-European world. The British Empire '"could encompass a great range of British interests, ambitions and sympathies", from militarists to humanitarians, feminists, missionaries, capitalists, scientists, and migrants'.[1] As has been seen in these pages, images of empire and the wider world came from a variety of sources. The impact on British culture of such images was uneven. Empire was often just a background feature, 'not a subject of popular political consciousness'. This fact, however, is remarkable in itself, for it meant that assumptions – about white people and non-white people, for example – were seldom challenged, and that millions of people grew up with an imperial mindset, inchoate though it might have been.[2]

The extent to which empire and stereotypical views of the non-European world were a part of the furniture of everyday life is the key theme reinforced in this book.

> With the exception of those in some official or quasi-official roles, for most people, empire was just there – out there. It was ordinary. Empire was omnipresent in the everyday lives of 'ordinary people' – it was there

as part of the mundane – of a familiar and pragmatic world which under normal circumstances, is taken for granted, neither questioned nor especially valued.[3]

The debate about the impact of empire on British culture, touched upon in the pages of this book, will continue. *Illustrating Empire* contributes to the debate by providing a rich array of primary source material drawn from the John Johnson Collection of Printed Ephemera in the Bodleian Library. It was this type of ephemera that was chiefly responsible for purveying to the British public a distinctly imperial view of the world, and of their place in it.

NOTES

INTRODUCTION

1. The phrase belongs to Reverend F.A. Walker and is taken from his 'Herodotus: How Far His Remarks Bearing on Egyptian Geology are Reliable in the Light of Recent Egyptian Research', *Transactions of the Victoria Institute* XXXI (1899), pp. 57-73.
2. Maurice Rickard, *Collecting Printed Ephemera* (Oxford: Phaidon, 1988), p. 7.
3. For a comprehensive biography, see M.L. Turner, *The John Johnson Collection: Catalogue of an Exhibition* (Oxford: Bodleian Library, 1971), pp. 5-18.
4. Graham Hudson, *The Design and Printing of Ephemera in Britain and America 1720–1920* (London: British Library; New Castle DE: Oak Knoll Press, 2008), p. 7.
5. Denis Judd, 'Picturing the Empire', *BBC History Magazine* 10/7 (2009), p. 70.
6. Flora Thompson, *Lark Rise* (Oxford: Oxford University Press, 1939); *Over to Candleford* (1941); and *Candleford Green* (1943), published together as *Lark Rise to Candleford* (London: Penguin, 1973).
7. Thompson, *Lark Rise to Candleford*, p. 193.
8. Ibid., p. 121.
9. Ibid., p. 181.
10. Bernard Porter, 'Empire? What Empire?: Imperialism and British National Identity, *c.* 1815-1914', National Europe Centre Paper no. 46 (Australian National University, 2002). The full flowering of the Porter perspective on empire, Britain and British culture is found in his masterful book *The Absent-Minded Imperialists: Empire, Society, and Culture in Britain* (Oxford: Oxford University Press, 2004).
11. Ronald Hyam, *Understanding the British Empire* (Cambridge: Cambridge University Press, 2010).
12. The debate between Porter and MacKenzie can be most readily accessed through their exchange in the *Journal of Imperial and Commonwealth History*. See Bernard Porter, 'Further Thoughts on Imperial Absent-Mindedness', *Journal of Imperial and Commonwealth History* 36/1 (2008) and John MacKenzie, '"Comfort" and Conviction: A Response to Bernard Porter', *Journal of Imperial and Commonwealth History* 36/4 (2008). MacKenzie has stated his case in other accessible essays, for example 'The Popular Culture of Empire in Britain', in Judith Brown and William Roger Louis (eds), *The Oxford History of the British Empire*, Vol. IV: *The Twentieth Century* (Oxford: Oxford University Press, 1999) and 'Another Little Patch of Red', *History Today*, 1 August 2005. Among a growing body of literature in this field, other works that stand out are Catherine Hall and Sonya Rose (eds), *At Home with the Empire: Metropolitan Culture and the Imperial World* (Cambridge: Cambridge University Press, 2006); Andrew Thompson, *The Empire Strikes Back? The Impact of Imperialism on Britain from the Mid-Nineteenth Century* (Harlow: Pearson, 2005); and Kathleen Wilson (ed.), *A New Imperial History: Culture, Identity, and Modernity in Britain and the Empire, 1660–1940* (Cambridge: Cambridge University Press, 2004).
13. Both published by Manchester University Press.
14. Titles from the Manchester University Press 'Studies in Imperialism' series that are of particular relevance to the subject of this book include Freda Harcourt, *Flagships of Imperialism: The P&O Company and the Politics of Empire from its Origins to 1867* (2006); Anandi Ramamurthy, *Imperial Persuaders: Images of Africa and Asia in British Advertising* (2003); and Stuart Ward (ed.), *British Culture and the End of Empire* (2001).
15. John MacKenzie, 'Popular Imperialism in Britain: Continuities and Discontinuities', draft chapter (2009), p. 2. Thanks to Professor MacKenzie for allowing us to see this work.
16. John Johnson Collection, Diorama 2 (16a)
17. John Johnson Collection, Diorama 1 (16).
18. John Johnson Collection, London Play Places 10 (7).
19. John Johnson Collection, London Play Places 10 (10).
20. John Johnson Collection, Food 5 (12).
21. John Johnson Collection, Empire and Colonies 1 (3), *Investors' Chronicle*, 30 May 1953.

ONE

1. Stuart Ward (ed.), *British Culture and the End of Empire* (Manchester: Manchester University Press, 2001), p. 4.
2. Figures from the *56th Report of the Postmaster General on the Post Office*, 1910, quoted in Andrew Thompson, *The Empire Strikes Back? The Impact of Imperialism on Britain*

from the Mid-Nineteenth Century (Harlow: Pearson, 2005), p. 60.

TWO

1. John MacKenzie, *Imperialism and Popular Culture* (Manchester: Manchester University Press, 1985), p. 3.
2. Randolph Churchill, *Winston S. Churchill*, Vol. I: *Youth, 1874–1900* (London: Heinemann, 1966), p. 545.
3. See Peter Hansen, 'Coronation Everest: The Empire and Commonwealth in the "Second Elizabethan Age"', in Stuart Ward (ed.), *British Culture and the End of Empire*.
4. For a comprehensive introduction to the imperial civil services, see Anthony Kirk-Greene, *Britain's Imperial Administrators, 1858–1966* (Basingstoke: Macmillan, 2000).
5. John MacKenzie, *Propaganda and Empire: The Manipulation of British Public Opinion, 1880–1960* (Manchester: Manchester University Press, 1984), p. 6.

THREE

1. Classic works on this subject include Edward Said's *Orientalism* (Harmondsworth: Penguin, 1978) and *Culture and Imperialism* (New York: Alfred Knopf, 1993), usefully read in conjunction with John MacKenzie's *Orientalism: History, Theory, and the Arts* (Manchester: Manchester University Press, 1995) and Bernard Cohn's *Colonialism and Its Forms of Knowledge: The British in India* (Princeton NJ: Princeton University Press, 1996).
2. Susan Thorne, 'Religion and Empire at Home', in Hall and Rose (eds), *At Home with the Empire*, pp. 164–5.

FOUR

1. Joanna de Groot, 'Metropolitan Desires and Colonial Connections: Reflections on Consumption and Empire', in Hall and Rose (eds), *At Home with the Empire*, p. 171.
2. Ibid., p. 174.

FIVE

1. The role of shipping and civil aviation in the British Empire has been the subject of numerous studies, including Harcourt, *Flagships of Imperialism* and Gordon Pirie, *Air Empire: British Imperial Civil Aviation, 1919–1939* (Manchester: Manchester University Press, 2009).
2. Figures from the *56th Report of the Postmaster General on the Post Office*, 1910, quoted in Thompson, *The Empire Strikes Back?*, p. 59.
3. See John MacKenzie, 'Imperial Propaganda Societies, and Imperial Studies', in MacKenzie, *Propaganda and Empire*; and Alex May, 'Empire Loyalists and "Commonwealth Men": The Round Table and the End of Empire', in Ward (ed.), *British Culture and the End of Empire*.

SIX

1. De Groot, 'Metropolitan Desires and Colonial Connections', p. 189.
2. MacKenzie, *Imperialism and Popular Culture*, p. 8.
3. MacKenzie, *Propaganda and Empire*, p. 3.
4. See Mike Cronin and Richard Holt, 'The Imperial Game in Crisis: English Cricket and the Demise of Britain's World Role', in Ward (ed.), *British Culture and the End of Empire*.
5. See Jeffrey Richards, 'Imperial Heroes for a Post-imperial Age: Films and the End of Empire', in Ward (ed.), *British Culture and the End of Empire*; and John MacKenzie, 'The Cinema, Radio, and the Empire', in MacKenzie, *Propaganda and Empire*.
6. See Brian Love, *Play the Game* (London: Michael Joseph, 1978); and *Great Board Games* (London: Ebury, 1979).
7. De Groot, 'Metropolitan Desires and Colonial Connections', p. 190.

SEVEN

1. See John MacKenzie, 'Imperial Exhibitions' in MacKenzie, *Propaganda and Empire*.
2. Quoted in MacKenzie, *Propaganda and Empire*, p. 106.
3. Thompson, *The Empire Strikes Back?*, p. 86.

EIGHT

1. Clare Midgley, 'Briging the Empire Home: Women Activists in Imperial Britain, 1790s–1930s', in Hall and Rose (eds), *At Home with the Empire*, p. 250. In the same volume, see also Antoinette Burton, 'New Narratives of Imperial Politics in the 19th Century'. Politics and empire is also covered in Thompson, *The Empire Strikes Back?*, and works such as Stephen Howe, *Anti-Colonialism in British Politics: The Left and the End of Empire, 1918–1964* (Oxford: Oxford University Press, 1993) and Bernard Porter, *Critics of Empire: British Radical Attitudes to Colonialism in Africa, 1895–1914* (Basingstoke: Macmillan, 1968).
2. Churchill, *Winston S. Churchill*, Vol. I, p. 259.
3. Bernard Porter, reviewing James Belich in the *Times Literary Supplement*.

AFTERWORD

1. S. Ward, quoting P.J. Marshall, *British Culture and the End of Empire*, p. 12.
2. Hall and Rose (eds), *At Home with the Empire*, p. 2.
3. Ibid., pp. 21–2.

FURTHER READING

Barker, Barbara (ed.), *Bolossy Kiralfy: Creator of Musical Spectaculars: An Autobiography* (Ann Arbor, MI: UMI Research Press, 1988).

Bell, Morag, Robin Butlin and Michael Hefernan (eds), *Geography and Imperialism, 1820–1940* (Manchester: Manchester University Press, 1995).

Boehmer, Elleke, *Colonial and Postcolonial Literature: Migrants Metaphors* (Oxford: Oxford University Press, 1995).

—— (ed.), *Empire Writing: An Anthology of Colonial Writing, 1870–1918* (Oxford: Oxford University Press, 1998).

Brantlinger, Patrick, *Rule of Darkness: British Literature and Imperialism, 1830–1914* (Ithaca: Cornell University Press, 1988).

Budd, Lucy, 'Global Networks before Globalization: Imperial Airways and the Development of Long-Haul Air Routes', *GaWC Research Bulletin* 253.

Constantine, Stephen, *Buy and Build: The Advertising Posters of the Empire Marketing Board* (London: HMSO, 1986).

——, *Emigrants and Empire: British Settlement in the Dominions between the Wars* (Manchester: Manchester University Press, 1990).

Coombes, A., *Reinventing Africa: Museums, Material Culture, and the Popular Imagination in Late Victorian and Edwardian England* (New Haven CT: Yale University Press, 1997).

Drayton, Richard, *Nature's Government: Science, Imperial Britain, and the 'Improvement' of the World* (New Haven CT: Yale University Press, 2000).

Driver, Felix, *Geography Militant: Cultures of Exploration and Empire* (Oxford: Blackwell, 2001).

Greenberger, Allen, *The British Image of India: A Study in the Literature of Imperialism, 1880–1910* (Oxford: Oxford University Press, 1969).

Greenhalgh, Paul, *Ephemeral Vistas: The Expositions Universelles, Great Exhibitions, and World Fairs, 1851–1939* (Manchester: Manchester University Press, 1988).

Hall, Catherine, and Sonya Rose (eds), *At Home with the Empire: Metropolitan Culture and the Imperial World* (Cambridge: Cambridge University Press, 2006).

Harcourt, Freda, *Flagships of Imperialism: The P&O Company and the Politics of Empire from its Origins to 1867* (Manchester: Manchester University Press, 2006).

Jackson, Ashley, *Mad Dogs and Englishmen: A Grand Tour of the British Empire at Its Height* (London: Quercus, 2009).

Kaul, Chandrika, *Reporting the Raj: The British Press in India, c. 1880–1922* (Manchester: Manchester University Press, 2003).

—— (ed.), *Media and the British Empire* (Basingstoke: Palgrave Macmillan, 2006).

Kohli, Marjorie, *The Golden Bridge: Young Immigrants to Canada, 1833–1939* (Toronto: Natural Heritage/Natural History, 2003).

Lahiri-Coudhury, Dhriti, *The Great Indian Elephant Book: An Anthology of Writings on Elephants in the Raj* (New Delhi: Oxford University Press, 1999).

Levine, Philippa (ed.), *Gender and Empire* (Oxford: Oxford University Press, 2004).

Lewis, Brian, *'So Clean': Lord Leverhulme, Soap, and Civilization* (Manchester: Manchester University Press, 2008).

Mangan, J.A., *The Games Ethic and Imperialism: Aspects of the Diffusion of an Ideal* (London: Routledge, 1986).

—— (ed.), *Benefits Bestowed? Education and British Imperialism* (Manchester: Manchester University Press, 1988).

—— (ed.), *Making Imperial Mentalities: Socialization and British Imperialism* (Manchester: Manchester University Press, 1990).

McCormack, Rob, 'Imperial Mission: The Air Route to Cape Town, 1918–32', *Journal of Contemporary History*, 9/4 (1974).

Macdonald, Robert, *The Language of Empire: Myths and Metaphors of Popular Imperialism, 1880–1918* (Manchester: Manchester University Press, 1994).

MacKenzie, John, *Propaganda and Empire: The Manipulation of British Public Opinion, 1880–1960* (Manchester: Manchester University Press, 1985).

——, *Orientalism: History, Theory, and the Arts* (Manchester: Manchester University Press, 1995).

——, 'The Popular Culture of Empire in Britain', in Judith Brown and William Roger Louis (eds), *The Oxford History of the British Empire*, Vol. IV: *The Twentieth Century* (Oxford: Oxford University Press, 1999).

——, *The Victorian Vision: Inventing New Britain* (London: Victoria and Albert Museum, 2003).

——, 'Another Little Patch of Red', *History Today*, 1 August 2005.

——, '"Comfort" and Conviction: A Response to Bernard Porter', *Journal of Imperial and Commonwealth History*, 36/4 (2008).

——, *Museums and Empire: Natural History, Human Cultures, and Colonial Identities* (Manchester: Manchester University Press, 2009).

——, 'Introduction', in John MacKenzie (ed.), *European Empires and the People* (forthcoming).

——, 'Popular Imperialism in Britain: Continuities and Discontinuities', in John MacKenzie (ed.), *European Empires and the People* (forthcoming).

—— (ed.), *Imperialism and Popular Culture* (Manchester: Manchester University Press, 1986).

—— (ed.), *Imperialism and the Natural World* (Manchester: Manchester University Press, 1990).

—— (ed.), *Popular Imperialism and the Military* (Manchester: Manchester University Press, 1992).

Midgeley, Clare (ed.), *Gender and Imperialism* (Manchester: Manchester University Press, 1998).

Nasson, Bill, *Britannia's Empire: A Short History of the British Empire* (Stroud: Tempus, 2006).

Opie, Robert, *Rule Britannia: Trading on the British Image* (London: Viking, 1985).

Pettitt, Clare, *Dr Livingstone, I Presume? Missionaries, Journalists, Explorers, and Empire* (Cambridge MA: Harvard University Press, 2007).

Pickles, Katie, *Female Imperialism and National Identity: Imperial Order of the Daughters of Empire* (Manchester: Manchester University Press, 2002).

Pirie, Gordon, *Air Empire: British Imperial Civil Aviation, 1919–39* (Manchester: Manchester University Press, 2009).

Porter, Bernard, 'Empire? What Empire?: Imperialism and British National Identity, *c.* 1815-1914', National Europe Centre Paper no. 46 (Australian National University, 2002).

——, *The Absent-Minded Imperialists: Empire, Society, and Culture in Britain* (Oxford: Oxford University Press, 2004).

——, 'Further Thoughts on Imperial Absent-Mindedness', *Journal of Imperial and Commonwealth History* 36/1 (2008).

Potter, Simon, 'Empire and the English Press', in Potter (ed.), *Newspapers and Empire in Ireland and Britain: Reporting the British Empire, c. 1857–1921* (Dublin: Four Courts Press, 2004).

——, *News and the British World: The Emergence of an Imperial Press System, 1876–1922* (Oxford: Clarendon Press, 2003).

Ramamurthy, Anandi, *Imperial Persuaders: Images of Africa and Asia in British Advertising* (Manchester: Manchester University Press, 2003).

——, *Black Markets: Images of Black People in Advertising and Packaging in Britain, 1880–1990* (Manchester: Manchester University Press, 1990).

Rich, P.J., *Elixir of Empire: English Public Schools, Ritualism, Freemasonry, and Imperialism* (London: Regency Press, 1989).

——, *Chains of Empire: English Public Schools, Masonic Cabalism, Historical Causality, and Imperial Clubdom* (London: Regency Press, 1991).

Richards, Eric, *Britannia's Children: Emigration from England, Scotland, Wales, and Ireland since 1600* (London: Hambledon & London, 2002).

Richards, Jeffrey, *Imperialism and Music: Britain, 1876–1953* (Manchester: Manchester University Press, 2001).

Riedi, Eliza, 'Women, Gender, and the Promotion of Empire: the Victoria League, 1901-1914', *Historical Journal* 45/2 (2002).

Said, Edward, *Orientalism* (London: Vintage, 1979).

——, *Culture and Imperialism* (London: Vintage, 1994).

Sebe, Berny, 'Celebrating British and French Imperialism: The Making of Colonial Heroes Acting in Africa, 1870-1939', D.Phil thesis, University of Oxford, 2007.

Spurr, David, *The Rhetoric of Empire: Colonial Discourses in Journalism, Travel Writing, and Imperial Administration* (Durham NC: Duke University Press, 1993).

Sugarman, Robert (ed.), *The Many Worlds of Circus* (Newcastle: Cambridge Scholars Publishing, 2007).

Thompson, Andrew, *Imperial Britain: The Empire in British Politics, c. 1880–1932* (Harlow: Longman, 2000).

——, *The Empire Strikes Back? The Impact of Imperialism on Britain from the Mid-Nineteenth Century* (Harlow: Pearson, 2005).

Tomkins, David, 'The Electronic Ephemera Project: Digitizing the John Johnson Collection', *The Ephemerist: The Journal of the Ephemera Society* 143 (2008).

Ward, Stuart (ed.), *British Culture and the End of Empire* (Manchester: Manchester University Press, 2001).

Webster, Anthony, *The Debate on the Rise of the British Empire* (Manchester: Manchester University Press, 2006).

INDEX